THE SOCIAL POLICY PROCESS IN CANADA

THE SOCIAL POLICY PROCESS IN CANADA

A. R. DOBELL
S. H. MANSBRIDGE

The Institute for Research on Public Policy/
L'Institut de recherches politiques

Printed in Canada

ISBN 0-88645-030-6

The Institute for Research on Public Policy/
L'Institut de recherches politiques
2149 Mackay Street
Montreal, Quebec H3G 2J2

A report of a Study by The Institute for Research on Public Policy,
and the Response to that Study, 1984-1985

CONTENTS

FOREWORD

The study documented in Part I of this report was undertaken as a first step toward a broader review of structural and institutional considerations bearing on the process of policy formation.

The study attempted a preliminary identification of the agencies and players involved in the social policy field, and their perceptions of the major questions to be confronted in the formation of social policy in the balance of the decade. The study did not purport to be a scientifically precise exercise in statistical inference, but it served to confirm the degree of sensitivity which attaches to several features of consultation processes and funding relations between governments and non-governmental organizations. It highlighted tensions with respect to possible links between lobbying activities and funding prospects, between advocacy and credibility, between openness and effectiveness in the consultation process for further research and debate. Furthermore, the findings suggested the need for more work on institutions for organizational consultation and collaboration, but more particularly, for flexibility and adaptability to regional and local conditions, as well as possible roles for Parliamentary Task Forces, for example, in the search for program innovations which rely more on imagination and design than on increased expenditures.

The Institute for Research on Public Policy undertook the study as part of its General Research Program, with financial support from Health and Welfare Canada. It did so, not in the expectation that this first pass would settle any questions, nor in the belief that the Institute was expert in the field of social policy, but with the conviction that both the current economic outlook and the changing expectations of many groups within the community impose a requirement for fundamental change both in the processes leading to decisions on social programs, and in the nature of those programs themselves.

The original Discussion Paper, of which Part I of this document is a condensed version, was completed by the end of 1984 and distributed to a broad sample of the organizations which had participated in the study. In the early months of 1985 reactions were received from several of these organizations; these, in turn, led to the decision to hold special meetings in Ottawa towards the end of June, not simply to discuss the original Paper but to determine what further initiatives were required to encourage action on some of the major issues which the study and the follow-up processes had identified.

Part II of this document describes the process of follow-up subsequent to the completion and distribution of the Discussion Paper. In particular, a number of important themes are described which reflect the changing dynamics of policy development; commentary is provided on the nature of social policy at this time, on networking and coalitions, and on the interface between non-government organizations and governments. Part II also includes reactions to the original Discussion Paper and the highlights of the June 1985 meetings covering participation, research and funding, as well as several proposals for future action in policy development.

The final draft of this monograph was completed before the Macdonald Commission reported the findings of its extensive review of economic and social policies. Of particular importance, in terms of the IRPP study of the Social Policy Process, is the reinforcement of the need to examine major policy questions in the broadest socio-economic context. Furthermore, the Commission's proposals for a complete restructuring of the Income Security field, and its advocacy of a

Universal Income Support Plan will demand a new approach to consultation with both governments and non-government organizations.

The Institute for Research on Public Policy might usefully play some catalytic role in this process of consultation on social policy formation. In particular, Institute staff hope to develop some mechanism to encourage examination of the conclusions on social policy outlined in the Macdonald Commission report by non-governmental organizations with primary interest in the realm of income security.

Further, IRPP may be one appropriate institution to initiate action on the widely-perceived need for new mechanisms in Canadian society designed to achieve a significant measure of integration in basic studies of economic policy and social policy.

The studies and the follow-up action described in this report owe a great deal to the effort and interest of a very large number of individuals. First and foremost, I wish to express my gratitude to the organizations and individuals participating in the original study, to those who provided valuable reactions to the original Discussion Paper and to the selected representative group which took part in two days of intensive discussions at the Ottawa meetings in June 1985.

Most of the structured work of the original study was performed by Darcy Coulson, Robin Goodrich and Allan Fuller, with assistance from Mervyn Brockett, Lauren Dobell and Rhonda Stoller. Mary Hegan carried out the major part of the follow-up planning, both in seeking and analyzing reactions to the Discussion Paper and in planning, implementing and identifying the highlights of the special Ottawa meetings. In this task, Shirley Seward provided valuable supervision and review. The study was carried out under the overall management of Stanley Mansbridge who was materially assisted by Martine Desbois, Dale Calvert and Heather Neufeld, particularly in the preparation of the discussion paper, supporting appendices and this Monograph.

We all recognize that the Institute has not, in this preliminary survey, produced definitive answers to the underlying questions relating to the Social Policy process, nor has it produced a blue-print for future solutions. I am confident, however, that with the help already provided by the participating organizations and individuals, and with their continued cooperation and involvement, a start has been achieved on a work program which can confidently be expected to make further progress and some useful contribution to the most fundamental contemporary problems of public policy in Canada. The Council of Trustees of the Institute has endorsed preparation of a longer-term work program for this purpose, and some continuing Institute contribution to the renewed debate on social policy set in train by the Macdonald Commission. Institute staff will welcome advice and assistance from all quarters in pursuit of this undertaking.

A.R. Dobell
President
Institute for Research on Public Policy

December 1985

AVANT-PROPOS

L'étude décrite dans la Partie I de ce rapport constituait, dans l'esprit de ceux qui l'ont entreprise, une première étape vers le réexamen plus général des considérations structurelles et institutionnelles qui entrent en jeu dans le processus d'élaboration de la politique.

Son objectif préliminaire était d'identifier les organismes et les acteurs intéressés à la politique sociale, et leurs perceptions des principaux problèmes à surmonter pour formuler une telle politique durant le reste de la décennie actuelle. Si elle n'avait pas la prétention d'être un exercice d'inférence statistique d'une précision très scientifique, elle a tout de même confirmé la présence d'un certain degré de sensibilité dans plusieurs aspects des processus de consultation et des rapports de financement entre les organismes publics et les organismes privés. Elle a mis en lumière les tensions occasionnées par l'existence de liens éventuels entre les activités des groupes de pression et les possibilités de financement, entre la défense d'une position et la crédibilité, entre l'élargissement et l'efficacité du processus de consultation, favorisant ainsi la poursuite des recherches et du débat dans ce domaine. Qui plus est, ses conclusions indiquent la nécessité d'effectuer des recherches plus poussées pour améliorer la consultation et la collaboration entre les organismes et, en particulier, leur flexibilité et leur faculté d'adaptation au contexte régional et local.

Elles suggèrent également la possibilité que les groupes de travail parlementaires puissent jouer un rôle important dans la recherche, par exemple, de programmes nouveaux qui mettraient l'accent sur l'imagination et la création plutôt que sur le simple accroissement des dépenses.

L'Institut de recherches politiques a entrepris cette étude dans le cadre de son programme de recherche générale et grâce à l'appui financier de Santé et Bien-être Canada. Il l'a fait non pas dans l'espoir que cette première tentative puisse régler un problème quelconque, ni dans la croyance que l'Institut était expert dans le domaine de la politique sociale, mais avec la conviction que la conjoncture économique actuelle liée à l'évolution des attentes de nombreux groupes au sein de la collectivité nationale rendent impératif un changement fondamental tant au niveau des prises de décisions en matière de programmes sociaux, qu'à celui de la nature même de ces programmes.

Le document initial, dont la Partie I de ce rapport est une version condensée, a été terminé à la fin de 1984 et distribué à un large échantillon des organismes ayant participé à l'étude. Plusieurs d'entre eux nous ont fait connaître leurs réactions au début de 1985, ce qui nous a incité à prendre la décision de convoquer des réunions spéciales vers la fin juin à Ottawa, non seulement afin de discuter du document, mais encore de déterminer quelles autres initiatives seraient susceptibles d'encourager l'adoption de mesures concrètes destinées à résoudre certaines des principales questions mises en lumière par l'étude et les travaux complémentaires.

La Partie II de ce rapport fait l'exposé des travaux qui ont suivi l'achèvement et la distribution du document. En particulier, on y trouve une description d'un certain nombre de questions importantes qui reflètent l'évolution de la dynamique du processus d'élaboration de la politique, ainsi qu'un commentaire à propos de la nature de la politique sociale actuelle, des réseaux et des coalitions, et des relations entre les organismes privés et les gouvernements. La Partie II fait également état des réactions provoquées par le document initial et présente les faits saillants des réunions de juin ayant trait à la participation, à la recherche et au financement, ainsi qu'à plusieurs possibilités d'action quant aux orientations futures de la politique.

La version finale de cette monographie a été achevée avant que la Commission Macdonald ne soumette les conclusions de sa grande enquête sur les politiques sociale et économique. En ce qui concerne l'étude du processus de formulation de la politique réalisée par l'Institut, on réaffirme la nécessité d'examiner les questions de politique dans un plus vaste contexte socio-économique. En outre, le fait que la Commission ait proposé une restructuration totale du programme de sécurité du revenu et recommandé un programme universel de soutien du revenu exigera que l'on découvre une nouvelle approche au processus de consultation tant avec les gouvernements qu'avec les organismes privés.

À cet égard, il est possible que l'Institut de recherches politiques puisse jouer utilement le rôle de catalyseur. En particulier, le personnel de l'Institut espère élaborer un mécanisme quelconque susceptible d'encourager les organismes privés à examiner les conclusions relatives à la politique sociale contenues dans le rapport de la Commission Macdonald, et notamment celles qui concernent la sécurité de revenu.

Par ailleurs, il se pourrait que l'Institut soit aussi l'organisme tout indiqué pour amorcer la découverte de nouveaux mécanismes, dont le besoin est largement ressenti, au sein de la société canadienne afin de parvenir à un certain degré d'intégration des études de base en matière de politique sociale et de politique économique.

L'étude et les travaux complémentaires décrits dans ce rapport doivent beaucoup aux efforts et à l'intérêt d'un très grand nombre de personnes. Avant tout, je tiens à exprimer ma gratitude aux organismes et aux personnes qui ont pris part à l'étude initiale, à ceux qui ont formulé de précieux commentaires sur le document de départ et au groupe des représentants sélectionnés qui ont participé aux deux journées de discussions intensives lors des réunions de juin 1985 à Ottawa.

Darcy Coulson, Robin Goodrich et Allan Fuller, assistés de Mervyn Brockett, Lauren Dobell et Rhonda Stoller, ont effectué la majeure partie du travail d'agencement de l'étude initiale. Mary Hegan était largement responsable de la planification des travaux complémentaires, tant au niveau de la recherche et de l'analyse des réactions provoquées par le document qu'à celui de l'organisation des réunions spéciales d'Ottawa et de la synthèse de leurs faits saillants. Shirley Seward a fourni un précieux travail de supervision et de révision dans l'accomplissement de cette tâche. Enfin, l'étude a été réalisée sous la direction générale de Stanley Mansbridge avec le concours matériel de Martine Desbois, Dale Calvert et Heather Neufeld, et notamment dans la préparation du document initial, des appendices et de cette monographie.

Nous sommes tous conscients du fait que l'Institut n'a pas pu, dans le cadre de cette étude préliminaire, apporter des réponses définitives aux problèmes sous-jacents au processus d'élaboration de la politique sociale, pas plus qu'il n'a formulé un plan susceptible de produire des solutions à l'avenir. Toutefois, j'ai la ferme conviction qu'avec l'aide déjà fournie par les personnes et les organismes participants, et avec la promesse de leur coopération et de leur engagement continus, l'Institut a accompli un premier pas vers l'élaboration d'un plan de travail qui, on l'espère avec confiance, pourra progresser et contribuer utilement à l'analyse des grands problèmes de politique qui se posent actuellement au Canada. Dans ce dessein, la Commission de direction de l'Institut a approuvé la préparation d'un plan de travail à plus longue échéance et le principe que l'Institut devra continuer à participer au débat sur la politique sociale, auquel le Commission Macdonald vient de donner une nouvelle impulsion. Afin de poursuivre ces objectifs, le personnel de l'Institut accueillera avec gratitude les conseils et l'aide de tous les milieux.

Rod Dobell
Président

SUMMARY

An important aspect of research on public policy is the assessment of the capacity of our institutions to respond to changing circumstances and to direct social forces toward an enhancement of the quality of life. In the Spring of 1984, therefore, the Institute for Research on Public Policy (IRPP), with the support of Health and Welfare Canada, embarked upon the first phase of an examination of the social policy process in Canada.

Social policy has been the subject of close scrutiny and intense debate in recent years. With the economic problems, and in particular the unemployment situation, posing serious challenges to governments and society, the demands and costs for social service programs are certain to be subject to increasingly critical review.

IRPP began its study in June 1984 with the preparation of a Background Note* which outlined the proposed scope of the study and undertook "to delineate in more detail the membership and activities of the social policy network." The study would also "open up the fundamental questions of how social policy analysis and advocacy can be coordinated and strengthened, and of the options available to governments to assist in achieving this objective."

* Appendix A to this Report.

The Note further stated that political and intergovernmental issues have implications for the consultation process: "The politically sensitive climate of federal/provincial relations, combined with the diffuse and decentralized nature of both federal and provincial social service departments, have posed serious dilemmas for program delivery agencies and social policy advocacy groups."

The study was intended to be exploratory and preliminary. Three months were taken to distribute questionnaires to a broad range of institutions, and to conduct interviews with a selected group of participants, and it was planned to have a Discussion Paper ready by the end of 1984 to serve as the basis for further review and discussion. More than 500 organizations, mainly non-government (NGOs), were provided with questionnaires, and some 62 individuals were interviewed. Detailed information on the Typology, the Methodology and the Questionnaire Analysis are provided in Appendices B, C and D to this Report.

The major themes for the study included: perceptions of the policy process; consultation--both with the public and with governments; funding of programs and organizations; the interface between senior government officials and heads of NGOs. The response to the preliminary study was most positive and demonstrated the need for and the timeliness of the examination of the issues.

In February 1985, following discussion of the first draft with Health and Welfare Canada, a Discussion Paper was completed by IRPP and distributed to the respondents to questionnaires and to participants in the interviews, and reaction was sought. Written and verbal responses were received which focused upon key concerns, the emerging social policy trends in a time of change and redefinition of public priorities, and possible solutions to the most pressing problems.

In June 1985, the IRPP convened a day-long meeting in Ottawa with fifteen individuals (representative of planning councils, interest groups, service organizations, business, labour, research groups, religious organizations, professional associations, and professional schools) and on the following day this group met with six government officials. The purpose of the two days of meetings was to provide a forum for a cross-section of representatives within the social policy network to examine the Discussion Paper and to develop reaction and direction. The discussions were informal and lively, informative and constructive, and resulted in many valuable suggestions for further action and--specifically--recommended a wide distribution of an IRPP Monograph embracing the original study, the reactions to it, and the highlights of the Ottawa meetings. It is this recommendation which has led to the production of this Report.

The Report is divided into two parts: the first part describes the preparation of the Discussion Paper and outlines its content in an abbreviated form. The second part covers the reactions to the Discussion Paper and the results of the Ottawa meetings, and may be described as the epilogue to the original paper. Appendices complete the Report.

ABRÉGÉ

L'un des principaux aspects de la recherche en matière de politique d'État consiste à analyser la capacité de nos institutions de réagir à l'évolution des circonstances et de centrer l'action des forces sociales sur l'amélioration de la qualité de la vie. Au printemps 1984, l'Institut de recherches politiques s'est donc engagé, avec l'appui de Santé et Bien-être Canada, dans la première phase d'un examen général du processus d'élaboration de la politique sociale au Canada.

Au cours des dernières années, cette politique a fait l'objet d'études approfondies et d'un débat très animé. Étant donné les graves problèmes économiques, et notamment le taux de chômage, que les gouvernements et la société doivent surmonter, il est inévitable que les exigences en matière de programmes de services sociaux, ainsi que les coûts de ces programmes, soient soumis à un réexamen de plus en plus critique.

L'Institut a commencé son étude en juin 1984 par l'élaboration d'une Note préliminaire* qui définissait l'envergure du projet d'étude et cherchait à "cerner dans le détail les membres et les activités du réseau de politique sociale." L'étude se proposait aussi de "mettre en évidence

---

* Voir Appendice A du présent rapport.

les questions fondamentales relatives aux moyens de coordonner et de renforcer l'analyse et les recommendations en matière de politique sociale et aux options qui s'offrent aux gouvernements pour favoriser l'atteinte d'un tel objectif."

La Note soulignait également le fait que les problèmes politiques et intergouvernementaux ont des répercussions sur le processus de consultation : "Le climat délicat des relations politiques fédérales-provinciales, conjugué à la nature diffuse et décentralisée des ministères des services sociaux, tant fédéral que provinciaux, ont placé les organismes chargés de l'application des programmes et les groupes militants en faveur de la politique sociale dans des situations souvent problématiques."

On voulait que cette étude soit de nature exploratoire et préliminaire. Il a fallu trois mois pour distribuer des questionnaires à un large éventail d'institutions et pour soumettre un groupe de participants sélectionnés à des entrevues. On projetait de rédiger un document qui serait prêt avant la fin de 1984 et qui servirait de base à la poursuite de l'analyse et du débat dans ce domaine. Plus de 500 organismes, privés pour la plupart, ont reçu des questionnaires et quelque 62 personnes ont participé à des entrevues. Des explications détaillées sur la typologie, la méthodologie et l'analyse des questionnaires figurent aux appendices A, B et C du présent rapport.

L'étude portait principalement sur les sujets suivants : les perceptions du processus de formulation de la politique; la consultation avec le public et le gouvernement; le financement des programmes et des organismes; les relations entre les hauts fonctionnaires de l'État et les dirigeants des organismes privés. Les réactions à l'étude préliminaire ont été extrêmement positives. Elles ont aussi démontré la nécessité et l'opportunité d'un examen des problèmes en question.

En février 1985, après avoir discuté du texte préliminaire avec Santé et Bien-être Canada, l'Institut a achevé un document qu'il a distribué aux répondants aux questionnaires ainsi qu'aux participants aux entrevues et leur a demandé de lui faire part de leurs réactions. Les réponses reçues, verbalement et par écrit, étaient axées sur les préoccupations clés, les tendances de la politique sociale qui se manifestent au cours de cette période d'évolution, la redéfinition des priorités publiques et diverses possibilités de résoudre les problèmes les plus urgents.

En juin 1985, l'Institut a tenu une réunion d'une journée, qui s'est déroulée à Ottawa, avec quinze personnes (des représentants de conseils de planification, de groupes d'intérêt, d'organismes de services, de groupements d'hommes d'affaires, de travailleurs et de chercheurs, d'organismes religieux, d'associations et d'écoles professionnelles). Le jour suivant ce même groupe a rencontré six fonctionnaires du gouvernement. On voulait que ces réunions constituent un forum où une tranche de représentants du réseau de politique sociale aient la possibilité d'examiner le document et d'élaborer des réactions et des orientations de politique. Les discussions ont été à la fois informelles et animées, informatives et constructives. Elles ont abouti sur un grand nombre de suggestions qui seront très utiles pour entreprendre de futures initiatives et, plus spécifiquement, sur la recommandation qu'une monographie de l'Institut, englobant l'étude originale, les réactions qu'elle a suscitées et les faits saillants des réunions d'Ottawa, fasse l'objet d'une très large diffusion. Le présent rapport est le fruit de cette recommandation.

Le rapport se compose de deux volets : le premier décrit l'élaboration du document et trace les grandes lignes de son contenu; le second est consacré aux réactions suscitées par le document et aux résultats des réunions d'Ottawa et peut être considéré comme l'épilogue du document initial. Le rapport se termine par des appendices.

PART I

SOCIAL POLICY PROCESS: THE DISCUSSION PAPER

Problems and Principal Players

For the purposes of the Study, the term "social policy" was broadly interpreted to correspond with current usage by Government, the policy, legislation or regulations enacted by the federal, provincial and municipal governments for the provision of social programs. More specifically, we interpreted social policy to be understood in the sense of the social policy 'envelope': consequently, our focus was to be broad enough to include the policy process relating to the Canada Assistance Plan, Education, Health, Veterans Pension and Allowance, Unemployment Insurance, Family Allowances, Old Age Security and GIS/Spouses Allowance, and Direct Programs falling within the scope of the social development spending of the federal government, including housing and employment programs. The federal social development budget in 1982-83 was $32 billion.

Transfers to "individuals" (covering payments to individuals, families with children, the unemployed and veterans) account for the single largest block of federal social expenditures, and form the core of the Canadian social security system. In 1982-83, the federal government spent 46 percent of its social budget on these programs; transfers to provincial governments for such major programs as health, post-secondary education and social assistance, represented about 27% of the social budget. Given the scale of the federal social budget expenditures and the impact on federal/provincial fiscal relationships, it is evident that, in times of constraint, the important issues of funding, programs, policy, roles and responsibilities assume overwhelming significance.

The "policy-makers" responsible in the parliamentary system of government for the elaboration of "social policy" are generally perceived to be the elected officials. At the same time, most Canadians would recognize that the elected officials necessarily work closely with senior public servants in the elaboration and consideration of social policy. The "target" for social policy development or social policy advocacy, by non-government organizations, is generally understood to include both elected and public service officials. The boundaries between politics, policy, programs and administration are often obscure. For the purposes of this Study, the Social Policy process consists of the complex web of interaction among politicians, public servants, the public and non-government organizations, leading to decisions affecting the provision of social programs.

In a report released by the Macdonald Commission, and dealing with Social Policy and Conditions, the section "Values and Public Attitudes" includes reference to a consistent concern that social and economic goals be better integrated in all areas of policy planning and development. Some submissions pointed out that, "in the past, economic and social goals were developed in parallel and often in isolation with little effort to integrate and to recognize their interdependence for meeting society's needs." The Economic Council of Canada noted that social goals and programs "...contribute fundamentally to the smooth functioning of our economy...our economic and social goals and programs are not separable; nor are social goals subordinate to economic goals."

The Background Note to the present Study* does not argue directly for an integration of social and economic policy process but it does suggest that the need for the Study is "...accentuated by a number of factors arising out of the present socio-economic context....Most important of these is the contemporary preoccupation with restraint in government spending", leading, for instance, to an interest in expansion of voluntarism and the voluntary sector, and "to removal of tax-exempt status for organizations engaged in political advocacy. This latter issue underlines the obvious hesitancy and ambiguity that exist with respect to the appropriate role of government in the funding, either explicitly or implicitly, of special interest groups in the social policy area." The Note compares this situation with that of the economic sector, where economic policy "is supported by a high level of interdepartmental, intergovernmental and private sector analysis and consultation. The study of economic issues is carried out by think tanks and research institutes, some of which rely on funding from government while others are privately funded..." The Note suggests that in the absence of a strong and well supported representation of the social policy voice of non-government organizations, narrow definitions of problems "...may lead in turn to overly specialized 'solutions' and result in a series of fragmented and uncoordinated government structures and programs." In times of economic growth, it would appear that governments in Canada functioned as though the economic prosperity of the country would more than cover the costs and requirements of necessary social program expenditures. In times of economic crisis and constraint, the evidence suggests the contrary. Many Macdonald Commission submissions expressed the view that in current circumstances, it is

---

* A copy of the Background Note is attached to this Report as Appendix A.

particularly important that the two policy domains, economic and social, recognize their interdependency and reciprocal impact.

The Background Note continues: "Economic policy formation draws representations from interest groups and coalitions acting in their own self-interest as economic agents. The underlying drive to influence economic policy towards general business objectives or specific sectoral objectives is the primary motivation for contributing to the general debate on economic policy. Moreover, research and commentary on economic issues can appeal to a well-developed, even though not universally accepted, body of macroeconomic theory and general principles of market mechanisms. Whatever the explanation for the imbalance in the level of applied analysis between the social policy sector and other policy sectors, the implications are not trivial. The danger exists that social policy concerns could be overwhelmed by the contemporary obsession with narrow indicators of international competitiveness and productive efficiency, leading to real deprivation for those less fortunate..."

Concerned with this imbalance between the social and economic sectors, the Note includes description of the present role and impact of non-government organizations involved in social policy analysis, discussion of the problems associated with the present systems of consultation and public participation in policy development, and explores the impact of federal/provincial co-ordination of social policy and funding policies on the activities of non-government organizations involved in social policy analysis and commentary. The Note implies that the strengthening and coordination of social policy analysis and advocacy is seen to be a positive goal, and that governments should be interested in examining options to achieve this objective.

The approach and style of government impacts upon the relative importance of non-government organizations. A government with a large majority may be less concerned with enlisting the support of interest groups or in enlisting their aid in winning support for providing advice on policy, whereas a minority government may instruct its public servants to promote the interest of pressure groups, to seek their advice, to ask for their assistance and to win their support. From time to time, interest groups or governments might seek the creation of a national or provincial organization for the purpose of enabling government policy and interest group objectives to coincide. The role of the interest or pressure groups, and those of senior government officials, become part of a complex web of relationships and interactions making up the policy process. Deputy ministers or senior officials, in examining and evaluating policy or policy proposals, in attempting to win support for policy options, and in bringing policy issues to the attention of the public, might consult with pressure groups or might, given the preference of the Minister of the day, choose not to do so. It can also be suggested that the extent to which a non-government organization provides important information or expertise to elected government officials or senior public officials determines to an extent "recognition". The Canadian Labour Congress and the Canadian Federation of Agriculture are invited to make presentations to Cabinet annually, as are some other organizations, thus winning status and membership credibility.

The Canadian Manufacturers Association was assisted in its founding by government officials, who saw a benefit in regular consultation, and the National Welfare Council, The Canadian Council on Social Development, The Vanier Institute of the Family, all benefitted from or benefit from some form of direct government encouragement. Some NGOs, which do not have the resources or expertise to provide authoritative advice to governments, are nevertheless given recognition for a number of reasons. Perhaps their constituency is broad, and politically significant, or they are recognized in order to give the impression of a balanced and representative, consultative spectrum, available to governments. For some organizations, recognition and government assistance are essential to credibility with membership.

Most Ministers would wish to be understood to favor consultation on policy, legislation or regulation, although each Minister might define the meaning of consultation differently. The Background Note suggests that the relative strength and effectiveness of the "social policy community" is relevant, and that governments would normally be interested in ensuring that the voice of the social policy community be expert, informed and effective. The extent of the influence on policy, legislation or regulation by non-government organizations depends on the attitude and preferred style of government and the government bureaucracy. Non-government bodies can find themselves in a "cooperative lobbying" role or an "adversarial lobbying" role, with major implications in either case. Some NGOs represent powerful interest groups which provide ample funding from within. The Canadian Labour Congress, The Canadian Manufacturers' Association, The Canadian Drug Manufacturers' Association, The Independent Petroleum Association of Canada, and the Canadian Medical Association, are all effective in serving the interests of their subscribing memberships, and are recognized by governments which seek their advice.

The Canadian Centre for Policy Alternatives receives no direct government support, is funded by its membership and activities, and offers membership to all who are interested. The Centre "recognizes the need for viable social and economic policy based on democratic control, public accountability, egalitarian principles and the right to meaningful employment." The National Anti-Poverty Association, the Canadian Hospital Association, Family Services Canada, The Canadian Council on Social Development, The Cooperative Housing Foundation of Canada, The Canadian Association for Adult Education are typical of organizations having a national character and mandate, although with differing membership, funding and structural profiles, and are typical of non-government organizations seen to be active in the social policy area and within the social policy community.

In Ottawa and the provincial capitals, there exist organizations for sectors such as business, labor, native people, educators, and health professionals. All look principally to their members' interests and seek to reconcile those interests with the national interest. The C.D. Howe Institute, The Business Council on National Issues, The Fraser Institute and the Canadian Chamber of Commerce are typical of organizations which are seen to be associated with business, but which cannot be said to be homogeneous as to orientation or perspective. For example, the Business Council on National Issues states that the Council "is not a lobby group seeking to represent narrow interests that have been traditionally associated with business. Rather the Council is dedicated to the fostering of public policies that will lead to stronger economic and social fabric within a healthy democratic society."

The Study was undertaken in 1984 when social and economic policy was in the spotlight, very much before the Canadian public and its political leadership. The health of the economy and the nature and effectiveness of many social policies and programs received the attention of political parties in the course of the federal election and the earlier leadership races. The federal government deficit, the Canada Health Act, Unemployment Insurance, the poverty line in Canada, the status of native communities, child welfare, child abuse, employment policy, are clearly part of the national agenda.

At the same time, the economic and business sector has raised the profile of business incentives, higher productivity, international trade, tax policies, and other issues arising from the declining economic well-being of the country. Significantly, voices from both the economic and social sectors could be heard speaking to both the business and the social perspective, and the national debate could be characterized as expressing a sense of profound concern with the need for change to deal effectively with both economic and social problems. More specifically, the Study was undertaken at a time when the following issues were prominent:

- the high level of unemployment, notably for the older worker and for youth;
- the impact of technological change on employment;
- availability of job training and the quality of vocational training;
- the problem of poverty, most notably for single parent families;
- the continued availability and quality of health care;
- economic strategies and options, notably from the perspective of their impact on employment;
- monetary policies and the impact of American budgetary and interest policies;
- the well-being of the Canadian family and Canadian children.

The study was carried out in three phases:

Phase One included preliminary planning and agreement on the terms of reference for the Study, with preparation of documentation and scheduling of interviews. An original sample of representative key contacts in the social policy field was prepared. Some 17 key contacts were invited to recommend to the Institute those organizations seen to be appropriate for the Study. A compilation of their recommendations produced a national listing, from which was selected a representative sample of individuals and organizations across the country for interview purposes. In addition, more than 500 organizations were identified as a target sample group to which a questionnaire was sent.

Phase Two involved confirmation of the interview respondent list, the arranging of interview dates and times, and completion of the interviews and reports. The interviews took place in August and September of 1984 and Interview Reports were completed by the end of September together with the preliminary analysis.

Phase Three included analysis of the material and preparation of the Report. (Further details of the methodology employed for the study are provided in Appendix B: Typology and Methodology.)

Historians have stated that the Fathers of Confederation could not have envisaged the present welfare state. The British North American Act (now the Constitution Act of 1867) did not clearly allocate social welfare responsibility to either the federal or provincial governments but, over time, responsibility devolved to the provinces because the Act referred to charitable matters and institutions as falling under provincial jurisdiction. Neither did the Act arrange for fiscal responsibility to match program responsibility. In practice, in the early years of Confederation, municipalities became responsible for poor relief, for charitable organizations, and for oversight of institutions.

The First World War caused the federal government to assume a greater social welfare role, notably for the dependent families of veterans, mothers' allowances, and basic public health services but municipalities remained primarily responsible for social welfare until the arrival of the Great Depression. The Rowell-Sirois Commission on Dominion-Provincial Relations recommended in 1937 a national unemployment insurance system and proposed that the federal government assume all or most of the responsibility for old age pensions. It confirmed provincial responsibility for health, social welfare programs and social insurance, for institutional health care, health insurance, and workmens' compensation. Most importantly, it clarified a number of important jurisdictional issues and laid a sound basis for future federal/provincial cooperation.

In 1940, a national Unemployment Insurance Act was enacted, followed in 1941 by the National Employment Service and, in 1942, a Committee on Health Insurance urged the reorganization of health services. In 1945, another watershed was established with the Federal Provincial Conference on Reconstruction. Its Green Book proposals included a declaration of national social purpose: "...to ensure for all Canadians high and stable employment and income and, secondly, individual economic security and welfare." It proposed assistance to private enterprise; involvement by government in public enterprise; job creation through public intervention; the taking of social welfare initiatives to deal with unemployment, sickness and old age; the creation of a national health care program, a national old age pension scheme, and extension of unemployment insurance.

In 1951, the universal old age security payments program was introduced for citizens of 70 and over, the Old Age Assistance Act provided support to those in need 65-70, and the Blind Persons Act was enacted. In 1956 and 1957, there followed the Hospital Insurance and Diagnostic Services Act and the

Unemployment Assistance Act and Federal/Provincial agreements on cost sharing of social assistance and hospital insurance programs were negotiated. In 1962, Saskatchewan brought in medical care insurance program, and, in 1966, the Canadian Medical Care Act, the Canada Pension Act and the Canada Assistance Plan became part of Canada's social policy history.

In the 1950s and 1960s, social policy development was characterized by federal/provincial cooperation but, in the mid-1970s, there was the failure to reach federal/provincial agreement during the Social Security Review. Attempts to salvage the cause of cohesive federal/provincial direction and cooperation failed again with the demise of the proposed Social Service Act in 1977. In 1984, the affordability of social programs, the effectiveness of the social safety net, and the universality of certain programs were under serious review.

Federal/provincial fiscal arrangements can be said to result from the dichotomy between provincial responsibility for many social programs and the vesting of financial powers with the federal government creating the need for a mechanism to permit the transfer of funds from the federal to the provincial jurisdiction. Although the federal government maintained responsibility for transfer payments to individuals, covered by programs such as Old Age Security, Guaranteed Income Supplement, Spouse's Allowance, Family Allowances, Unemployment Insurance, and Veterans Pensions and Allowances, the transfer of funds to the provinces constituted 27% of the social budget in 1982-83 for programs such as health, post-secondary education and social assistance.

The Parliamentary Task Force on Federal-Provincial Fiscal Arrangements was established in 1981 to provide parliamentary input into the 1982 review of fiscal arrangements. It reviewed the Federal-Provincial Fiscal Arrangements and Established Programs Financing Act and the Canada Assistance Plan, dealing notably with fiscal equalization, established programs financing, and federal/provincial tax collection agreements. It is the Federal/Provincial Fiscal Arrangements and Established Programs Financing Act which authorizes the two major transfer programs: fiscal equalization, and established programs financing. The Act is the principal vehicle for transfer of funds from the federal level to the provincial level of government. The purpose of equalization is to assist those provinces with below-average revenue to finance basic government services without being obliged to raise taxes above the national norm. Equalization payments are unconditional. The Established Programs Financing Act provides for "block funds", (cash or tax transfers) for the funding of such programs as medical care, hospitalization and post-secondary education.

The Canada Assistance Plan provides for federal cost sharing with provinces for social assistance and welfare services. The cost-sharing is in two major areas: (1) social assistance for those in need, covering food, clothing, shelter, fuel, utilities and supplies, funerals, and for some health costs, such as drugs; (2) welfare services, including rehabilitation; counselling; child welfare services; assessment and referral services; homemaker and day care services; research; and some provincial costs of service delivery. Conditional cost-sharing, conditional grants, and direct federal funding provide the federal government with influence and a degree of control although the programs require provincial cooperation, agreement or coordination. Block funding, tax revenue funding and direct provincial or municipal funding gives greater control to the provinces and municipalities.

The machinery of federal/provincial liaison includes formal Federal/ Provincial Conferences and Committees which are varied in their mandates and membership. Some are continuing committees, others ad hoc in nature, and time limited. Most are composed of Ministers and/or officials who discuss issues of common interest and concern. Secretariat services are usually provided by the Canadian Intergovernmental Conference Secretariat, an organization funded by all elven governments. In addition, there are Interprovincial Committees which are formed as consultative and information-sharing bodies, and are often used to determine joint approaches for negotiations with the federal government.

The First Ministers' Conference, chaired by the Prime Minister, is the most senior body and is concerned with policy at the highest level on matters of importance for all governments. The Constitutional Conference is the plenary conference of Prime Ministers and Premiers called to deal with constitutional issues, and there is a Continuing Committee of Officials which reports to the Constitutional Conference. The Tax Structure Committee of Ministers acts as a task force and examines the allocation of tax resources among governments, and the Federal-Provincial Continuing Committee on Fiscal and Economic Matters is a committee of senior officials dealing with fiscal and economic matters. Finance Ministers meet annually to discuss the financial and economic situation and to attempt to harmonize fiscal and economic policies.

Some federal departments have regional offices with the mandate to facilitate regional intergovernmental cooperation and communication. Federal/provincial committees are often created in regions, but with varying degrees of flexibility and delegation. Experienced federal and provincial administrators agree that it is the informal, day-to-day contact, the telephone calls, the personal visits, which do most to ensure positive and constructive liaison. However, the effectiveness of this liaison is influenced to a great extent by the prevailing political relationships between the two orders of government. Many provinces have established Inter-Governmental Agencies to help coordinate their relationships with other governments and to facilitate internal communication, so essential to effective coordination of public policies within and between governments.

There are also a number of committees for sectors and areas of interest, such as agriculture, resources, industry, manpower, education. For example, the Energy and Resource group includes a Canadian Council of Resource and Environment Ministers, somewhat unique as a corporate association of ministers. A number of Advisory Councils are appointed under federal statute or order-in-council to advise various ministers and when these Councils include formally designated provincial representatives, they can function as federal/provincial committees; one such example is the Canada Health Council. The Institute of Public Administration of Canada is an example of a non-government organization, (a professional association) which can serve as a vehicle for communication and consultation, particularly among officials of all levels of government, as well as universities.

As noted earlier, the municipalities carried at one time the major responsibility for social programs and services. Today, the role of the municipalities varies from province to province and the argument that Canada boasts of ten social systems has some validity, for the differences among provinces are significant. There are, nevertheless, important players in the social policy and social service field at the level of the regional governments and the social planning councils. Many respondents in this study have referred to the high quality social policy analysis and commentary produced by these social planning councils.

The history of the Canadian system of government reveals a capacity to build upon federal and provincial interaction, and central and regional juxtapositioning of themes and issues. If, as many have argued, the role of the largest Metropolitan and Regional governments is to be increasingly important in the Social Policy Sector, one consequence would be the demand for participation in social policy planning at the federal and provincial levels of government.

Roles and Perceptions

This section describes the attitudes and perceptions of the participants in the policy community and analyzes the implications for the consultation process. Participants are divided into policy advocates and government officials. The officials were senior officials of line departments (federal, provincial and municipal) responsible for aspects of social policy development and administration within their jurisdictions and departmental mandates. The policy advocates are the non-government players, the individuals in various types of non-government organizations which have specific social policy goals.

Sometimes advocates are referred to as "lobbyists", but this term no longer seems to apply since NGOs attempt to influence other NGOs as often as they do government officials -- hence the use of the term "advocate". Some non-government respondents may be uncomfortable with the label of "policy advocates"; in this context however, the term is meant to identify those people in non-government organizations who are involved in pursuing various social policy concerns of interest not only to their immediate members or constituents but also to the general public. Although a strong element of self-interest may be present, the recommendations of social policy advocates are aimed at social change on behalf not only of their organization's members but also on behalf of special groups in society who are disadvantaged and in need of government assistance. Policy advocates, in this sense, are members of a wide variety of organizations operating at every level of jurisdiction in all policy fields. Their approaches to policy influence vary widely, from high profile media campaigns to quiet, indirect infiltration of the policy agenda with research and networking, and to organizing and supporting local self-help programs and community organizations. Their proposals may be explicitly goal or issue oriented, and may be aimed indirectly at the process of consultation and consensus building.

It is important that government officials recognize certain characteristics and attitudes prevailing amongst those working actively in the social policy field. Social policy advocates generally see themselves as concerned with the human side of the policy agenda, with issues they consider to have been neglected for political reasons or dominated by economic considerations. Backgrounds in experimental work and community-oriented development activities provide some organizational sophistication; yet "the system" itself is often blamed for the hardships experienced by the members or clients of the NGOs for whom the advocates work. The gaps between the administrative culture and the client-oriented cultures sometimes give rise to misunderstandings which confirm a perception of officials as servants of systems rather than people, responding to rules rather than ideals.

Information is difficult to obtain and the policy and decision-making processes of government are rarely explained or debated. Advocates complain that official feedback and follow-up are unusual, departmental mandates divide "problems" into pieces which do not fit the needs of individuals, funding support is often short-term, usually inconsistent, and seems to be tied to constraints on policy activism. The individuals attracted to social policy advocacy are interested in reforming what they perceive to be "wrong-headed" policies and legislation. They are prepared to work long hours, often for little or no pay, and without public recognition.

Policy officials and politicians should be actively seeking the perceptions and advice of this network, as part of the process of national concensus building and as a way to discover regional sensitivities and alternative methods of programme delivery. But it is important to recognize the differing backgrounds, cultures, and belief systems of many of those involved, and the different organizational needs of small groups of non-specialists working on very limited budgets. Resources and advance notice must be provided to NGOs in order to facilitate their timely and well-researched participation in the policy process. Officials and politicians could also encourage social policy NGOs to "build bridges" with other policy players by funding projects, seminars, and workshops where these organizations are exposed to the priorities of representatives of business, labour, and academic communities. The present efforts at "consultation" offer some valuable experiments in this respect.

At the municipal level, administrators of social planning or social service departments most often portrayed themselves as service-oriented, close to their communities and prepared to take on a major role in social policy development. Criticisms of federal and provincial or federal interdepartmental bickerings were sharp, and the "emerging role" of municipalities was a constant theme. Local officials spoke about the need to tailor social services to local conditions and often seemed to identify with the dilemmas of NGOs facing reduced budgets and lack of access to the provincial level of government. A strength, as far as municipal administrators are concerned, is the fishbowl environment of local politics: aldermen and city councillors are available, meetings are generally public, and officials are instantly accountable. NGOs were generally perceived as "service delivery agents", with credibility and experience regarding the community impact of programs, and therefore as allies in the lobbying process.

The overall flavour of responses from municipal officials was relatively pragmatic and optimistic, focussed on the role of local leadership and community development, and on working closely with voluntary agencies to maintain an appropriate level of family and individual services.

In some ways, municipalities are in an enviable position. Their status as creations of the provincial governments provides them with a convenient scapegoat for reductions in service when provincial restraint programs are in place. Local politicians, public meetings, and close working relationships with funding organizations, such as the United Way, provide opportunities to receive sensitive and accurate information regarding the wants and needs of their communities and reduce the gap between elected representatives and officials. The concentration of many municipalities on "community development" has created links among business organizations, politicians and voluntary agencies that have resulted in reasonably "integrated" social and economic policy making. Municipal officials profess a positive attitude towards consultation with NGOs, but tend to see NGOs as useful to them only at the program delivery stage. Given the administrative role of the municipal governments themselves, and their distance from federal and provincial policy centres, this is not surprising. The involvement of many municipalities with national organizations, such as the Canadian Council on Social Development, was described as useful because of the information produced by the council for policy discussions between municipalities and other organizations, particularly where these added to the repertoire of municipal arguments for federal/provincial/municipal negotiations, funds for local projects, and increased sensitivity to local problems.

The "public interest" is defined by municipal officials as the needs of their city or community, and sometimes as the needs of cities in general. Rural needs and national standards did not arise, except in the sense that city officials could picture a "broker" role for municipalities between federal and provincial priorities. Employment, especially for youth, the health of local businesses and industries, and the needs of families and the handicapped were emphasized. Sound management, local design and delivery, and the rationalization of social policy responsibilities among governments were goals that were stressed. Local officials with knowledge of federal and provincial political and bureaucratic processes reported an ability to harmonize federal/provincial policies and delivery of services at the local level. Local officials rarely mentioned political ideologies, unless prevailing philosophies appeared to lead to arbitrary social policy decisions and dysfunction, secrecy or hostility in the consultation process between provincial governments, municipal governments and NGOs. When this occurred, local officials tended to be critical of provincial "paranoia".

Local officials are likely to be supportive of NGOs that:

(a) fill an obvious service or information need in the community;
(b) demonstrate an interest in local decision-making and pursue that objective in their presentations to federal and provincial governments; and
(c) demonstrate an ability to communicate with local politicians and the local business elite, viz: the "policy community" at the municipal level.

Jurisdiction in the social policy field dictates a process of on-going negotiation between provincial governments and the federal government. Provincial officials in social service departments reported a sense of vulnerability to public opinion and media manipulation because of the public perception of social policy as program delivery and therefore a provincial responsibility. Provincial officials frequently felt that federal officials were insensitive to regional needs.

The "public interest", according to some provincial officials, is served by keeping the Minister well informed, and by seizing the opportunity resulting from "recession management" for forging stronger links with NGOs prepared to take a tactful, businesslike approach to the trend towards privatization of services. The emphasis from these respondents is on the responsibility of the political level for policy making and the importance for NGOs of good research, a credible volunteer base, membership funding and a concern for delivery of services. NGOs with supporters in the business community were seen as particularly credible. Inconsistencies among the provinces in the degree of openness to NGO influence may indicate that styles of consultation are a factor which has permeated from the political to the official level. NGOs who lobby are likely to be seen by provincial politicians as operating outside the legitimate political stream, and therefore the onus is on them to be "politically smart", community based, and able to present their positions with data and cost impacts included. Media involvement is considered prejudicial to effective lobbying of government.

Federal officials pointed to problems of interdepartmental coordination and inter-branch rivalries, the absence of consistent regional input into social policy, and an absence of vision and leadership, particularly in the social service field. A persistent "underdog" attitude prevails when some officials compare the status of their departments with the central agencies and economic development departments. There was need to review the economic and social policy interactions of the federal and provincial governments. Some officials, especially those with responsibilities for both the social and economic needs of certain populations (e.g., natives), were noticeably more enthusiastic about the potential of the local level for policy planning. NGOs in the field (with the exception of health lobbies) are viewed as disorganized and inconsistent in both approach and quality of analysis.

The federal officials interviewed for this study were members of line departments, at the levels of Deputy Minister, senior ADM and ADM. Their policy role is to bring new initiatives into the upper levels of the policy community. Here, at the senior political and administrative levels (the Cabinet and the central agencies), social and economic policies are identified, priorized and coordinated. The department that demonstrates a capacity to help the government achieve its priorities is in a strong position to justify increased status and resources; this leads to a great deal of competition among departments to produce programs related to the latest policy agenda. At various times, national unity, multiculturalism, regional expansion, and citizen participation, for example, have elicited program responses from departments, rarely coordinated and each with its own collection of supportive and/or critical

NGOs (Pross, 1980). Senior officials devote considerable energy to the competition between line departments for space on the policy agenda of the central agencies.

Studies have shown that officials in the central agencies (PCO (including PMO and FPRO), Treasury Board Secretariat, the Department of Finance, Office of the Comptroller General) have taken a remarkably isolationist stance towards "outsider" input (Campbell, 1983). Compared to their British and American counterparts, Canadian officials in central agencies demonstrated the least interest in obtaining the views of outsiders, and fell behind in consultation with business and union leaders, local government officials, religious leaders, leaders of ethnic groups, citizen groups and other professionals.

Clearly, line departments are in a position to "own" the consultation process with NGOs. By providing core and project funding, information, access to officials, support for conferences, workshops, seminars, and appearances before task forces, Royal Commissions and Committees of the House and Senate, a dependency relationship is established. Social policy line departments are the only channels for input by NGOs at the federal level, but the policy agenda in recent years has been dominated by economic issues. Departments which are seeking to enhance their importance in the overall structure of government by making in-roads on the policy turf of the central agencies are likely to provide extensive support to organizations that provide economic analysis of policy issues. Social services, a "cost" item in the eyes of most economists, have not been a recent priority for the federal government, and it should not be surprising that NGOs that consider such services a priority have not been well funded relative to economic policy NGOs. At the level of individual departments, senior officials described their frustration with current policy development processes. This may be because power is in fact diffused throughout the public service, rather than delegated. Few levels and fewer individuals have the capacity to cut through federal and interdepartmental and intergovernmental red tape and actually initiate a positive response to a policy problem (Pross, 1980).

For NGOs, these comments raise the following concerns:

(a) Consultation can occur for many reasons, including both genuine policy concerns, the organizational needs of the department and the political needs of Ministers. NGOs should be aware of and be sensitive to these imperatives, which are characteristic of large, complex, political organizations.

(b) Central agencies are relatively untouched by social policy NGOs. This implies that NGOs must tread carefully but persistently to access these additional centres of authority, without jeopardizing their present working relationships with line departments.

(c) Time and money spent on a credible NGO image and thorough research are resources well spent. Senior officials appreciated analysis of their policy intiatives, particularly in light of what they see as a gap in the "program expertise" level in their own and provincial analytic ranks.

NGOs repeatedly referred to their "communication" function, not only with government departments and politicians regarding the concerns and reactions of their members or target group, but also to the recipients of government programs and to the general public regarding the needs for various policies. It may be inferred from this observation that NGOs are carrying out these functions because government departments with social policy responsibilities are unable to communicate directly and effectively to the public at the operational level, or to relay local concerns efficiently through departmental channels to the decision-makers.

A policy or program that cannot be understood by its beneficiaries is unlikely to be effective. NGOs are constantly involved in explaining and accessing government reports and programs on behalf of the individuals they represent. The amount of "service to the public" extended to thousands of people by NGOs is clearly a benefit to governments that often seem unable to untangle the current maze of programs intended for people in need and entitled to services. When a problem occurs or a new need emerges, the average individual is unlikely to have the time, resources or expertise to sort through the administrative or political channels that may or may not exist to receive and resolve the issue. This is an essential function of interest groups and one that is particularly necessary in the social policy field, where identified needs are often urgent and basic.

The reactions of NGOs may be an efficient and politically expedient substitute for lengthy and expensive program evaluations. This has mixed implications, given that many NGOs are highly dependent on government funding and may find their survival threatened when their advocacy activities become embarrassing to a government or department. However, accurate feedback from NGOs regarding the unintended impacts of government policies will be invaluable, if coordination of the complex range of social and economic programs aimed at certain populations (women, the poor, natives, the disabled) is attempted. Canadian policy development is traditionally a process hidden by layers of confidential interdepartmental and intergovernmental negotiations. One of the most important roles of NGOs in policy development may be the opening up of that process to scrutiny by citizens who have interests and experience in specific fields, and to the general public. This is accomplished not only with the usual formal and informal lobbying tactics of NGOs, but also through the role these organizations play in obtaining and disseminating the reports and analysis produced by government in the various policy fields. Without NGOs (and the media), a great deal of this information would simply circulate internally within government and would not become part of the process of "informed public debate".

Most NGO representatives spoke about a federal "culture of consultation", reflecting their experience of being able to access federal officials fairly readily. However, the groups that noted this were also well aware that in their fields of interest, the federal government was not paramount and that their advocacy activity was probably influential only in the degree to which it allowed the federal government to influence provincial programming through demonstration projects. These projects are used not only to highlight certain needs (e.g., women's studies, health, transition homes, community programs for the mentally ill), but also to enhance "federal visibility". However, groups that rely directly on departments for programs that are administered federally (for example, co-op housing), or rely on federal leadership (for example, natives), reported only slightly better responsiveness from federal departments than is being experienced from provincial governments by regional organizations. It may be that as jurisdictional authority for a given problem is clarified, consultation actually becomes more problematic.

NGOs also identified a role for themselves in terms of providing continuity in social policy development, which they feel is not now provided by rotating Ministers or by career administrators. Many representatives felt a bond of common interest with the federal and provincial officials involved in the "building era" of the 60s and early 70s, when most of the present government frameworks for social policy delivery were constructed. This was not only an extended period of growth and prosperity but also an era in which many federal social policy officials and departments had strong connections with provincially regulated community agencies. In the current climate of 'economic siege', heads of social policy NGOs feel isolated and ignored. There is a sense that new professionals in government have come from backgrounds in economics and business administration. In many provinces, large social service agencies have been replaced by government departments, and the private/government exchange of professionals no longer occurs. NGOs may, therefore, be providing "continuity" but the danger is that it is a continuity of language and perceptions that is of interest only to themselves. In one sense, this is a valid networking strategy and builds alliances that respond well to a crisis or an issue on a task force agenda. On the other hand, on-going communication with officials and politicians is the real source of NGO influence, and ways must be found to overcome current communication barriers.

The Funding of Social Policy Development

The Study briefly examined the important issues of funding as part of the review of the social policy process in Canada. The scope of the Study did not allow for intensive analysis of all social policy funding, nor of the effectiveness or content of social policy activity but permitted comment from a number of perspectives.

The Pattern of Funding

Respondents have suggested that responsibility for social development in the federal and provincial governments is, correctly in the view of many, diffused throughout the mandates of many departments rather than one or a few. This would imply that responsibility for social policy is equally diffused throughout government and the same would be true for funding responsibility. Indirectly, funding for social policy activity is provided by any department which budgets for it, or which supports or funds policy or research activity under departmental auspices. This Report will describe funding of NGOs only, funding which is allocated specifically and directly to NGOs having social policy interests, and which are significantly engaged in social policy activity.

Federal Government Funding

Many of the NGOs which participated in the study looked for funding to Health and Welfare Canada, CEIC, or the Secretary of State, and the funding takes two forms: sustaining grant or project funding. Funding can support a broad range of interests, from social services to minority group development to multiculturalism.

In the broader meaning of the term 'social policy', all research grants issued for education, health, veterans, income security, family allowance, unemployment insurance or their social development programs can be seen to be social policy development funding if used for policy analysis or research, publication or education activities.

Funding Sources

Whereas the administration of funding programs is complex, the criteria for decisions unclear, decisions are sometimes arbitrary, perhaps politically oriented, the sources of funding multitudinous, and the competition for funding fierce, somehow the system is seen to be relatively effective. However, in some provinces, cutbacks have obliged NGOs to close their operations; for example, in Calgary, the Social Planning Council ceased operations due to inadequate funding. Most funded NGOs have felt the impact of reduced funding.

Funding grants usually go to support operations and research within the mandate of the funder, leaving many NGOs in a position of having to find outside funds or abandoning more comprehensive and holistic research or policy analysis. Most funding is short term, while effective research, notably community-based and evaluation research, is long term. The absence of multi-year funding for some NGOs makes it impossible or at best risky to pursue other than 'dollar-driven' research, although some seek and find alternative funding.

Few officials or NGO officers could describe the scope of funded research or the total funding provided. There is a sense that investment by numerous authorities in government is significant, but the total and the benefits are not known, implying the need for some form of information gathering mechanism or a secretariat to collate the benefits. However, it is recognized that research results are owned by the funder, and are not necessarily available to others. In times of constraint and reduced funding, and a demonstrated need for more relevant research for contemporary problems, there is a tendency to look for rational management in the management of research. It is suggested by many that to avoid conflict of interest which could be engendered by undue control of research goals and content by funding sources, a third party vehicle could be considered. This suggestion does not imply the need for a single research office but rather an office for the gathering of information on research, and the dissemination of the results of research. A "clearing-house" function providing information to NGOs as well as government agencies might improve the effectiveness of research efforts already under way.

General Comment

Whereas the respondents acknowledged the legitimacy of governments or organizations wanting to pursue research for their own purposes, and the right of governments to fund research according to their own priorities, they also identified the need for independent research and advocacy. There is acknowledgement that no initiative is value-neutral, but that "independent research" is essential. Nor is this view held only by NGO officials, as some of the most eloquent arguments for independent research were made by senior federal government officials.

Many respondents, notably those engaged in service delivery, have found that service and program evaluation research or research funding is not available despite the fact that, in their view, policy validation occurs at the delivery level. They believe that delivery agencies must become more involved in policy development based on program and service evaluation studies, if policy is to be other than politically or administratively rationalized; the client is seen by them to be the reason for the policy.

Coordination and cooperation among levels of government was seen as an issue by many respondents. There were many examples of successful joint ventures between two or three levels of government, although the majority of cases involved municipal and federal governments. Generally, provincial governments are not committed to research. With the emergence of the city and city-related planning departments or social planning councils, the importance of city funding of local research, with or without federal or provincial involvement, is increasingly acknowledged. As cities and provincial governments become more engaged in "management of the public sector", there will evolve an increased interest in research and data collection to enhance the quality of management and municipal decision-making and a possible equivalent interest in wanting to control that research.

Many respondents expressed disappointment that the social service academic community had not developed appropriate interest and expertise in practical, applied and other research in the social policy sector. The example given is the failure to demonstrate the benefits or cost effectivenes of social welfare funding. Instead, the community seems to have hidden behind ideological arguments about the inappropriateness of applying management criteria to "soft" products. Many respondents insist that all public investment requires validation and if the social science leadership will not produce justification for the programs it has endorsed, perhaps we need a new generation of social economists.

On the issue of funding with 'strings', a number of viewpoints were expressed. Some argued strongly that any government involvement in research and policy analysis becomes suspect whereas others suggest that responsible government involvement entirely or in part is a necessity. Most agreed that NGOs should move towards a mixed funding base to include revenue derived from fee for service work, from government and others. Some argue that governments should not evaluate their own programs, or hire private firms to do

- 18 -

so. Evaluation should be undertaken by disinterested third party organizations, such as NGOs, where the process could be relatively open and consideration of the best and most viable options become a subject of public knowledge and discussion. There is general acknowledgement that the study of social policy is underfinanced in comparison to the economic sector and that within the social policy sector social welfare is the most neglected. This acknowledgement is made in the context of a major crisis for many Canadians, due to unemployment and related issues, and that the present social programs are not designed for that kind of general social dysfunction. Funds must be found to initiate solid research on the strengths and weaknesses of the present programs and policies, and on the direction which should be pursued for the next several years.

One frequent theme was the need to accept the premise that all interest groups are value-laden, have a viewpoint and an interest to pursue. There is a sense that any NGO purporting to pursue the national interest is, in fact, merely pursuing what its own leadership believes to be the national interest. It is suggested that NGOs should be more honest or objective about what it is that they intend, and then proceed to search for funds from those of like mind, rather than the general public or government. Interest group or single issue NGOs seem to function more successfully.

Most support the argument that there is need for a review of the federal government's grant administration, mainly to ensure that the criteria currently used and the societal needs are consistent, but there are few suggestions as to what model to adopt or what changes to make. Many suggest that there is a language problem with respect to such concepts as social policy, consultation, research, affordability, social needs, validation and evaluation. One reason for supporting a national social policy forum or socio-economic national forum would thus be to validate the language, the values and the concepts.

The Process of Consultation

As noted earlier, the formal creation of the Canadian federal state through the British North America Act (the Constitution Act of 1867) involved a distinct division of powers and responsibilities. The federal government was to work within certain spheres of influence, and exercise certain roles, and the provincial governments were to act within certain prescribed parameters, the two to be complementary. The dual federalism which resulted soon gave way to the more pragmatic 'give and take' of the current political model, because the rigidity implied in the concept of "watertight compartments" was unworkable.

The participation phenomenon of the last two decades has affected private enterprise, government and citizens at large, and there is an expectation that employees and citizens will be involved in decision-making through participation in planning, impact analysis, policy review and other organizational or political exercises. However, in the view of some public administrators and political executives, the majority of citizens are not in favour of interest group involvement in the government process, and would be reluctant to see government encourage participation, given the possibility that pressure group influence could favour specific interest groups over the citizens at large. In addition, the increased interest of public administrators in strategic planning and policy, programs and budget planning -- and more particularly, increased appeal to massive data sets and elaborate information processing for policy debate -- would seem to make more difficult any significant participatory or open decision-making process.

Citizens and the non-government organizations they support will nevertheless press for some form of participation because of a concern that the complexity of government and the scope of decision-making are such that public awareness, scrutiny and participation are essential. There is some distrust of government by experts because of a lack of sensitivity among such experts to the impact of decision-making in the public domain. Because of the dynamic tension between the two views it is likely that agreement will be reached on new forms of participation which will permit efficient management of government and yet allow citizens and NGOs to contribute and cooperate within the process.

The problem of "unforeseen consequences" of decision-making in a centralized, large public system requires some form of effective public participation. At issue, perhaps, is the readiness of both government and NGOs to look at and to try new ideas and options. The leadership style of the late 1980s will be effective to the extent that it brings together relevant resources and people in an enabling and facilitating decision-making and policy process in place of a closed, expert, directive leadership style.

During the course of the interviews conducted throughout the study, attention was directed to discussion of how consultation is perceived and understood, the nature of the structures and processes governing consultation, and the effectiveness of the process. Some of the more pertinent observations which arose are listed here:

(a)   Important though lobbying is seen to be, including active relations with the media, there is concern that funding (usually from governments) can be jeopardized.

(b)   Undue reliance on government funding can clearly be a limiting factor on the independence and objectivity of an NGO.

(c)   The consultation process is made more difficult given the overlap and at times the conflict, among the various levels of government involved with social policy.

(d)   There was inadequate public reporting and debate on social policy issues and insufficient briefing of the business and labour communities. In consequence, the process of consultation with these vital groups in society is weak and largely unproductive.

(e)   Important regional and major metropolitan forms of government are frequently overlooked in the consultation process although they are often the most knowledgable of both needs and program impact in the social policy field.

(f)   A major factor affecting the initiation of consultation is the particular set of values and attitudes possessed by the participants.

(g) It is an important role of governments to ensure that the full range of views is heard on public policy issues and objectively examined.

(h) NGOs require information from governments as to the location of decision-influencing and decision-making offices so that representation can be efficiently directed.

(i) Information is a vital element in effective consultation and access to all relevant data in the social policy field must be unrestricted.

(j) There is objection to the frequent "closed-door" nature of federal/provincial policy reviews and a strong belief that representation of NGOs in such reviews is both desirable and necessary for acceptable policy conclusions.

(k) The most needy in the public realm are the least involved when social policies are debated.

(l) At the core of most of the inadequacies in the consultation/participation process is the inadequate funding of the social policy organizations outside of governments. As noted above, however, undue reliance on governments for funding has its own serious limitations. Other solutions must be sought.

NGO Networks and Trends

The social policy network of NGOs is constantly changing its players, their roles, their power, and the relationships of players to each other and to governments. As social policy is redefined to meet emerging needs, and with federal, provincial, and municipal governments modifying their roles and responsibilities for social programs, the non-government network of players becomes more complex. The dynamics of the field make it difficult to obtain a comprehensive and detailed picture of the social policy network at a national level. What is both possible and necessary however, is to understand the dynamics and trends in the system so that all interested players might work effectively together.

Non-government groups interested in addressing social policy form a multi-levelled matrix with four conceptually distinct categories based on government counterparts (municipal, provincial and federal) and on a combination of purpose and intention of the group. There are services or 'theme' groups, which have a priority focus on one area within the broad social policy "envelope", such as income for the poor, health, housing, education, crime prevention, social rights, justice. There are the groups which address the range of service areas in terms of the special needs of their members; these include groups serving women, the disabled, youth, seniors, visible minorities, organized workers, and consumer groups. Thirdly, there are the regional or community-oriented groups which speak for the combined social needs of people from geographical and culturally unique areas, such as social planning councils, district health councils, and community development groups. The fourth category in the matrix is represented by the professional associations, professional schools, and research groups, which influence policy from an "expert" perspective.

Impact upon policy development is greatest when these different levels and arms form a consensus, coalition, or alliance around specific themes, policies or programs. While most networking and coalitions in the social policy field are formed in response to government agendas and funding decisions, a number of recent liaisons and networks have been forming around non-government agendas. The reason for this is that NGOs are searching for solutions that existing government institutions seem unable to offer.

In addition to collective group action, social policy is influenced by individuals using such means as polling, expert input, personal contact with politicians and officials, and individual commentary through the media. Emerging technology and communication systems are also increasing the capacity of governments at any level to carry out referenda and other forms of individual consultation. Media, research publications, pollsters, and groups skilled in public awareness and public relations play an increasingly important role in the social policy network. To some extent, they control the information and contacts that are essential for all groups and individuals who seek to influence policy choices.

Government and non-government funding bodies indirectly impact upon and form part of the social policy network. Government grants and funding programs influence the role and possibly the freedom of NGOs in policy development because of the predominant need for, and the conditions associated with, such funding. Private foundations, United Ways, service clubs, corporate and union funders also express social policy interest and sometimes social policy preferences through selection of the NGOs they fund.

Certain national voluntary and professional organizations have played established, long-term roles in social policy development. For example, the coalition of National Voluntary Organizations (NVO) addresses those national issues (e.g., tax reform, definition of charity) that affect the overall operation and 'raison d'etre' of voluntary groups in society. The National Voluntary Health Agencies (NVHA) include approximately 18 large, national voluntary organizations which work closely with National Health and Welfare. Other federal departments in the social policy envelope have established similar umbrella, coordinating groups to address their key ongoing responsibilities. However, the overall NGO network for any one department or federal minister is expanding beyond established voluntary organizations and professional associations to include policy groups in the labour and business sectors and among special interest and consumer groups. An example of one such emerging and influential group is the local community development corporation.

The most visible linkages between groups and sectors are the established coalitions, with memberships enjoying regular, joint meetings amongst staff and/or volunteers, co-sponsored conferences, and shared newsletters. Some of these interactions, reflecting common interests and resources, develop their own identities, structures and unique roles for the purpose of social policy development. For example, in 1979 a broad range of groups concerned about the erosion of medicare met at a national conference and formed the Canadian Health Coalition that now has its own constitution, office, and provincial affiliates. Since most issues and programs in the social policy field involve federal and provincial jurisdictions, and can include municipal implementation, coalitions often develop locally and in each province. Alliances and networks are most easily and quickly coordinated at a community level to meet emerging current needs. They often develop into information-sharing advocacy bodies which in turn group with similar bodies to attempt to influence provincial and national decision-making.

Cross representation amongst Boards and standing committees of different organizations provides another link in the social policy network and arises in order to increase the availability and exchange of information; no formal inter-organizational relationship is necessarily implied in such arrangements, however. As with coalitions, such liaison occurs at local, regional, provincial and national levels of existing organizations and government institutions. Within service and issue areas there are formal links and coordinating bodies to bring together professional and service associations with consumer groups, and with other related groups which speak for certain interests of society as a whole. Examples include: senior citizen councils at the local level; provincial coordinating and advisory bodies; and national groups such as the Canadian Council on Social Development (CCSD), National Associations Active in Criminal Justice (NAACJ), and the National Day Care Association. Government advisory bodies and major government Task Forces and Commissions often bring different sectors together for common concerns, may formalize linkages between themselves and NGOs, and may spawn non-government coalitions around issues.

Ongoing networking and informal contacts among individuals and groups with similar interests, provide the necessary cohesion to the social policy network, and fuel much of its dynamism. Activists interested in social policy often hold responsible positions in religious organizations, voluntary groups, self-help and/or special interest groups and it is often these individuals who wear "a number of hats" locally, provincially, and federally in different sectors and organizations, and who integrate ideas, contacts, and working relationships. Such fora as political party meetings, Institute discussions, think-tank groupings, can also play an important role in the social policy network as a source of new ideas and different points of view. These informal linkages provide a support system, a testing ground for new ideas, a sharing of essential information, that formal structures may otherwise withhold, and the building of trust and respect that can assist consensus-building. Such linkages can also centralize power and control among a few individuals and government contacts. If formal organizations and coalitions are not strong, organized, and openly accessible, then informal groups may try to fill the gap by doing business with governments informally, or by forming new advocacy movements.

As in any social movement, it is those leaders who emerge with the support of both the formal and informal networks who determine which organizations will play a central role in policy change. Umbrella organizations and coalitions have taken turns, and have sometimes competed to be the key spokesmen for social policy with politicians and the media. Because of the diverse backgrounds and perspectives of players in the social policy field and because of the field's volatility, the balance of power often moves among NGOs. Yet, most recognize the need for joint action in order to change policy and to provide leadership in a changing world. The democratic process among the three levels of government can slow down the development of policy, but the informal networks can help quicken debate and coalesce energies for action.

There are several emerging trends and changes within the social policy network, of which the following are significant:

(a) Informed consumers are forming and joining special interest groups whose prime interest is to play a key role in defining and choosing the best possible social programs and policies to meet the range of social and economic needs. Often, consumer groups originating at a local level form provincial, national, and even international organizations in order to address different levels of government responsibility. The desire to be self-reliant and to exercise control of service delivery encourages consumers to participate in groups and coalitions separate from established voluntary organizations and government-related institutions. Some new consumer groups are challenging the established structures (professional associations, research bodies) for equal representation in consultation with governments. However, when governments and other NGOs recognize the importance and validity of consumer input, then many consumer groups welcome formal partnership arrangements with non-consumer organizations.

(b) There is an increasing call to "humanize" and "personalize" social programs to meet local community needs and, when added to greater consumer participation, there is pressure to develop national and centralized social policy from the "bottom-up". This augments the desire for more direct local participation with national policy makers and challenges the traditional provincial approach whereby municipalities and local branches of tri-level NGOs speak only to their provincial structures, which then carry the burden of participating in federal-provincial discussions. This process also puts pressure on federal officials to appreciate local needs and not just rely on provincial contacts. Modern communication systems encourage information-sharing, and facilitate cross country-discussions amongst communities.

(c) Out of a desire to achieve more global, holistic, and integrated planning, social concerns are being debated within a broader economic and environmental context and this necessarily will involve a broader range of players in the social policy debate. Increasingly, social needs (e.g., employment, child care, housing) are being addressed from socio-economic perspectives and involve economists as well as social planners, business and labour as well as the social delivery system, and embrace local economic development as well as social and health planning. Furthermore, in times of service rationalization and public funding restraint, a broader range of groups and sectors become indirectly involved in social policy decisions as program and funding trade-offs are made amongst and within levels of government.

(d) Many government departments develop relationships and ongoing consultation with the NGOs most relevant to their areas of responsibility. Federal government decision-making on social policy involves not only the Department of Health and Welfare but, the Finance Department, Employment and Immigration, Regional Economic Development, the Secretary of State, etc., and these government Departments have broadened the consultation base of contacts and NGO advisors. Business, labour, and special interest groups are also being asked for opinions on social policy as key players in the socio-economic debate.

(e) With changes in government come new waves of consultation and consensus-building. Players with different attitudes gain access to power and so do different groups and organizations. As governments introduce new consultation processes, the policy network must modify its negotiating strategies, its relationships, and its informal liaison with government.

(f) There is believed to be growing public concern about the extent of government involvement in day-to-day living and in the provision of services to meet all human needs. Consequently, some NGOs are seeking greater independence in provision of programs and, rather than waiting for government initiatives, are attempting to develop new policy initiatives through multi-sector liaison and problem-solving studies.

(g) Given the Charter of Rights, and the increasing interest in securing equality and justice through constitutional rights, groups will seek to affect social policy and social program delivery through court decisions or the threat of legal action. Some members of the social policy network are updating their knowledge of legal procedures, combining resources and strategies to solve social inequalities, and are seeking equal access to services through legal rather than merely legislative decisions.

(h) There is a significant increase in the direct interest of Unions in social conditions in society at large and in action towards exercising influence in policy changes.

Observations and Possible Courses of Action

The great variety of NGOs militates against the possibility of a uniform point of view. Differences arise among national organizations, between national and provincial groups, and among groups operating at the local or regional levels. NGOs differ in the extent to which they seek to influence programs rather than policies, as to whether their spokesmen believe contacts with politicians to be more productive than with officials, and as to the importance of close personal relationships with those seen to be most influential in the making of policy or the development of programs. Nevertheless, some general concerns can be inferred from the responses to questionnaires and the views expressed during interviews.

Some NGOs are concerned that social progress in Canada is at risk, due to an apparent polarization of the business/government sector and the less powerful social sector, and many seek a commitment to the making of decisions on social and economic policies through an open government process.

The Native Peoples and Social Policies

It would have been impossible within the time constraints of this study to have carried out a thorough examination of the particular issues involving the native peoples and their representative non-government organizations. It would also have been inappropriate, given the special status of the native peoples and the important discussions in which their representatives are engaged with the federal and provincial governments on constitutional issues and issues of the machinery of government.

Nevertheless, a few discussions were held with NGOs representing native peoples. In these discussions, the over-riding importance of the current constitutional discussions was emphasized whilst, at the same time, recognition was accorded to the very particular importance of social policies among the native communities throughout Canada. In any follow-up action taken as a result of this report, it will be essential to take into account the special needs of native people.

Non-Government Organizations

Representatives of NGOs, perhaps because of their limited resources and the tendency to focus on the holistic needs of particular groups of people, appear to be less aware of the social policy-making machinery of government and how best to influence that system than one would expect. The best example of this apparent lack of awareness is the fact that, consistently, NGO representatives appeared to be only superficially aware of the intricacies of federal and provincial agreements with regard to social policy development and program funding, although these agreements are fundamental to social policy in Canada. Although secrecy surrounds these arrangements, NGOs need to know these mechanisms and the people responsible for them, intimately: otherwise the position of NGOs will always be reactive, fulfilling an important but peripheral role as watchdogs at the program delivery stage.

If NGOs were to decide to focus on the development of social policy, their target Ministers and departments might be priorized somewhat differently. In addition to the usual departments, targets would include central and economic development agencies, provincially and federally, and influential NGOs in fields other than social policy: e.g., business lobby groups, schools of Economics, research institutes, and political party policy analysts. Their message would be concerned with the costs and benefits of social programs, both to the economy and to individuals, the social responsibilities of the business community, and the investment-incentive value to a country or province of a strong system of social safety nets. The emphasis would be on how to organize communities for full social and economic recovery and on the role of social policy NGOs in bringing normally adversarial bodies together, i.e., business and labour, federal and provincial governments.

The data base for costs and benefits of social programs is weak and program evaluations are sporadic and often insufficient. The role of target groups as consumers (e.g., the disabled, the elderly) is not well documented and as social services are privatized, cost and quality comparisons are not routinely developed. These are examples of information needs that are time-consuming and expensive to address, but are essential for a business-like approach to social program justification. Many NGOs may be non-partisan, with the necessary community and professional resources to conduct some of the basic surveys and studies that are needed, but some are not prepared to abandon their "moral position" in order to pursue objective information. Business and economic research groups have long known the strategic power of putting a dollar figure to a program proposal, indeed to argue the cost/benefit ratios: this is a reality that NGOs in the social policy field cannot afford to ignore.

Social programs have long been viewed as residual-affordable only if the economic climate is favourable. The experience of the recession has brought home the necessity for an adequate social safety net for individuals during periods of prolonged unemployment. However, the belief that "individual effort" is really at the root of success or poverty and deprivation is also a basic cultural belief. Social programs are expected to provide a minimum standard of living, not to replace individual initiative. The growing interest in better "targetting" of social resources, as opposed to maintaining universality, is an indication of disbelief in the effectiveness and manageability of monolithic social programs. NGOs need to acknowledge this trend, and to stress their ability to detect opportunities for regional and local "tailoring" of social programs.

NGOs in the social policy field are seldom involved in initiating contacts outside their usual circles of sympathetic groups and individuals and this tends to result in polarization of views, often in ideological terms. Some cooperation does occur, of course, most often with joint projects focussed on job creation, and with municipal and provincial government support and federal funding. Additionally, individuals with overlapping memberships in the business and social policy networks initiate some contact, and the MacDonald Commission also brought normally opposed bodies into some consultative sessions.

Further, it might be argued that the members of the social policy network have to define their own roles and strategies and that, in order to sustain involvement in the process of policy development, NGOs must share information with each other and with their members. The struggle for a secure existence is likely to result in a more aggressive and business-like approach to fund raising, more mergers and coalitions, and a greater emphasis on fee for service activities.

Effective NGOs will learn from the health lobby and the business community, will increase their understanding of the language and agendas of the prevailing political regimes, and will seek to build networks of contacts with a variety of departments. An example of this is the "inside constituency" of the women's organizations, which effectively utilizes formal interdepartmental committees and processes to affect the policy agenda.

Effective federal officials, with strong regional contacts, will insist that NGOs be able to demonstrate fiscal accountability through knowledge of the grass roots they claim to represent and an ability to relate to many types of interest groups and institutions. This can be achieved by focussing on regional concerns, developing working relationships with local universities and local agencies, and obtaining support from the provincial and local business communities and governments.

Federal/Provincial Relations

Most respondents regretted the apparent decline of federal/provincial cooperation, and the absence of a joint commitment to pursue a common vision, despite partisan interests. It is expected, however, that governments will succeed in improving relations and in conciliating differences, but there is concern that the need for a continued strong federal role might be sacrificed for cooperation and conciliation.

Discussions and agenda planning for federal/provincial meetings should be made known to the public and to NGOs, and the recent practice of closed discussion should be abandoned. It is argued that the people of Canada are ready to engage in a public debate on social and economic futures and are prepared to recognize and accept the current harsh realities with a view to cooperating in finding meaningful and effective solutions. Furthermore, the majority reject the right/left ideological polarization as artificial and insist that the differences are mainly of emphasis and approach. There is expectation that the new federal government will continue the main elements of the social contract, but will examine possible modifications. The probability of continued serious unemployment presents the major reason for enhanced federal/provincial cooperation, and provides the primary stimulus for joint study of social and economic issues.

The Processes of Consultation

Few NGOs are satisfied with the processes of consultation now being followed, although there is recognition that the prevailing economic malaise throughout Canada has a major effect on the scale and quality of consultation which might usefully occur, particularly when compared with the climate which obtained one to two decades earlier.

It is argued that authentic consultation requires equal access to the information base of the subject-matter, and sufficient time for the information to be studied and evaluated. It is clear that effective consultation does sometimes occur, in the experience of NGOs, and that some governments are more forthcoming and successful than others. Similarly, the attitude of some NGOs, in their communication with government representatives, is more conducive to candid and useful joint exploration of issues than is the unduly aggressive and argumentative approaches of others. It is apparent from both government and NGO responses in this study that all sides of the consultation framework could usefully re-examine their particular attitudes, having as the primary goal a determination to make the most effective possible contributions to the solving of social policy problems.

Consultation based upon internal working or policy papers, "after the fact" consultation as many believe it to be, is much resented. Individual NGOs, or coalitions of NGOs concerned with specific policy issues, believe that involvement in policy development or modification should be continuous, if their relevant knowledge and experience are to be adequately utilized. In other words, effective consultation must include participation in problem definition and in the design of policy responses. There is a widespread belief that the consultation process needs to be defined, that the definition should be the subject of considerable care and exploration by an appropriate and respresentative body, and that the resultant definition should be adopted by all levels of government.

Social policy-making suffers, it is argued, when its major focus is seen to be exclusively the needy, the poor and the powerless. Instead, social policy should address the total community, and its objective should be the prosperity and well-being of all citizens. NGOs in the social welfare field will achieve greater policy influence to the degree that they succeed in achieving identification with an informed citizenry. In this regard, there is an evolving view of the need for a broadening of perspective of both the social and economic policy agencies of government, and the non-government organizations, leading to a measure of integrated socio-economic analysis and policy development. This issue is referred to again in a later section of this part of the report.

Research and Funding

The strong interconnection of independent research and adequate and secure funding has been frequently emphasized by NGOs in the social well-being field. Few NGOs are satisfied with the adequacy or the quality of the limited research they are able to perform, and almost all NGOs are conscious of the shortage of funds available for good research. Furthermore, when the source of funding is primarily government, many NGOs are conscious that research can hardly be fiercely independent, particularly if the research results were to appear to be over-critical of the funding source. It is not surprising that many social policy NGOs regard with envy the relative richness of NGOs in the economic sector, and their apparently well-endowed research activities. This "poor-relation" position is further aggravated by the conviction that the inter-relationship of the economic and social fields is axiomatic, that society's objective should not be prosperity or welfare, but the prosperous social well-being of the total constituency.

The majority of the respondents engaged in service delivery operations considered that the most serious gap in research was in evaluation of programs and services, and that policy and program validity must necessarily be tested at the point of delivery: indeed, the absence of such program evaluation made it difficult if not impossible to validate policy and program design. Furthermore, many NGO spokesmen believe that government program evaluation, with a set of jointly agreed criteria, could most effectively be carried out by carefully selected NGOs and that the revenue earned through such contracts would serve as an important and desirable source of earned revenue for the NGOs.

Again, from the perspective of many NGOs, the research conducted at present is fragmented, uncoordinated, usually very short-term, and ineffectively supervised and evaluated. On the other hand, the social policy field is in need of major pro-active research on a much longer-term basis in order to facilitate "direction-finding" for the purpose of achieving consensus on socio-economic objectives. In this regard, a case was made for an approach similar to certain corporate R&D practices, whereby "revenue generators and revenue spenders" (in this context, the public and private sectors) would cooperate in developing research strategies and effective research control.

Many NGOs recognize that self-funding would be preferable to government funding and that adequate funding would permit competent and effective research. Furthermore, several NGOs are conscious of their numbers in what are frequently narrow fields of interest. It is recognized that the competition for scarce funds, whether for essential overheads or limited research, might be less painful if coalitions of interest groups could lead to mergers, with a consequential increase in influence and research capacity.

There is some interest in the concept of new research groups evolving in the social policy field and acting independently of the special interest NGOs, provided that effective consultation can take place on research activities and that an appropriate commitment of funds is made to assure excellence, continuity, and security. In this regard, it was recognized that institutions such as IRPP or CCSD might properly perform an independent research and coordinating role in the social policy sector, on behalf of social policy NGOs, whilst, at the same time, providing at least the initial and desired bridge between the social and economic sectors.

Questions of Organization

Several NGOs regretted the absence at the federal level of a unifying high-profile social policy authority. Too many departments and agencies had a piece of the social policy 'pie' and this fragmentation of responsibility precluded a rational framework for policy formation. In fact, the fragmentation led to the widespread attitude of 'defending the policy turf'. Furthermore, the absence of an integrating authority made more difficult the performance of the important national role of protecting and enhancing the social progress achieved to date throughout Canada. To a lesser extent, similar difficulties in achieving a unified social policy approach were noted at the provincial government level and for similar reasons. Of equal concern in this connection, however, was the absence of an efficient instrument for inter-provincial policy review. A strong case could be made not only for the development at each level of government of a social policy entity to strengthen analysis, assure legitimacy, and facilitate policy development, but also for the collectivity of provincial governments to create a Provincial Secretariat for Social Policy Analysis and Development with which national NGOs and the federal authority could consult on an on-going basis.

Another emerging concern noted by several NGOs was the function of social planning at the level of the major cities and metropolitan regions across Canada and the emergence of active and energetic Social Planning Councils or Departments. It was argued that provincial governments seldom seem to recognize the particular and severe impact of economic adversity on the cities, and that there is inadequate consultation on the social welfare measures which are needed and the program evaluation which is required. Again, the absence of an integrating authority for social policy development at the provincial level makes unnecessarily difficult the pursuit of effective dialogue between these two levels of responsibility.

Socio-economic Policy Planning

As noted earlier, many practitioners in the social policy field, at the national, provincial and regional levels, are concerned with the aparent dominance of economic analysis and research and the relative neglect of social policy. To over-simplify the issue, it is believed to be inefficient and inappropriate to continue these two solitudes, one believed to be occupied with the making of wealth and the other with its distribution, and it is contended that these two policy sectors need to coalesce.

There are many ways in which this objective, if it were accepted, could be met; it is possible, for example, to construct a spectrum of alternatives ranging from a simple beginning, requiring a modification or redefinition of an existing institution, to the creation of a major new organization. The spectrum can be illustrated by the following four 'milepost' possibilities:

(a)   An existing institution, such as the IRPP -- whose terms of reference are indeed broad enough for the purpose -- could be targetted by the broad membership of the social policy sector to fulfill the need for a new consultative framework, and become the vehicle for research and public debate on social and economic issues. It would be essential to involve government, business and labour along with the social policy NGOs in such a joint venture on policy development. At the same time, the institutions involved would need to pursue the cooperative partnership of the private and public players in the social and economic spheres, and in the process of socio-economic modelling.

(b)   Alternatively, an agency such as the Economic Council of Canada could be reconstructed as a Socio-Economic Council. Given that the existing Council is a creation of the federal government, it would be necessary to consider modifications to assure the new Council being seen to be representative of all levels of government as well as the principal national NGOs, and to be staffed and funded to permit adequate examination of the social policy sector.

(c)   It might prove possible to redirect the work of one or more of the major economic boards or institutions, now largely constituted to represent the economic interests of the private sector, to embrace the broader responsibilities of socio-economic analysis, research and policy development, and to serve the much enlarged constituency of public and private sector social and economic interests.

(d)   A national conference, appropriately convened and representative, could be called to design a new Canadian Socio-Economic Council whose purpose would be to provide fully integrated research, analysis and policy development in the economic and social policy realms of Canada.

Follow-up

Representatives of several organizations have emphasized the importance of this IRPP Study at a time of fiscal restraint and economic difficulties, and have noted its timeliness given the election of a national government mandated to re-examine policies and programs and to enhance cooperation with provincial governments. There was equal endorsation of the need for follow-up action on the findings of this report, including a special seminar of representative delegates to discuss the report and its findings and proposals.

Conclusion

This is perhaps the first time in Canada that a descriptive study of the Social Policy Process had been attempted, with a particular focus on the role and impact of non-government organizations, and of the particular difficulties encountered by these organizations in seeking to influence government policies and programs on behalf of their respective constituencies.

This report has emphasized the preliminary, indeed exploratory, nature of the study in what is clearly only the first phase of a most necessary, important and timely examination of the subject. Nevertheless, the study has been able to identify a number of critical issues among which are:

- the inadequacies of the process of consultation involving governments and NGOs, and the imperative need to achieve agreement on what consultation means and how it is to be undertaken;
- the need for more research of high quality in the social policy field and for more efficient research structures;
- the organizational barriers within and between the various levels of government and the need for innovative approaches to a number of organization changes which are needed;
- the serious funding problems of the organizations which seek to protect and serve client populations, particularly those whose clienteles are among the most weak and the most poor;
- the existence of what the report refers to as "two solitudes", the mainly separate fields of Social Policy Analysis and Economic Analysis, to the detriment of truly effective policy planning in these inter-dependent policy sectors.

The report recognized that follow-up action would be needed, first to test and extend the findings from the study and thereby to define more precisely the policy issues to be confronted, and subsequently to bring the results to bear on current discussions of economic policy.

When the Discussion Paper (of which Part I of this Monograph is an abbreviated form) was distributed early in 1985, comment was invited. In addition, special meetings were convened by the President of the Institute for Research on Public Policy in June 1985 to review and discuss the feedback and the possibility of further action. Part II of this Monograph reports the re-action to the Discussion Paper and the highlights of the June meetings.

REACTION TO DISCUSSION PAPER, AND HIGHLIGHTS OF MEETINGS

JUNE 25-26, 1985

A Summary document and the full Discussion Paper were distributed early in 1985: from March to May, 34 individual responses (written and verbal) were received. Respondents included 10 government officials and 24 NGO representatives, from all regions of the country, who provided national, provincial and local perspectives. The reactions focussed upon key concerns, emerging social policy trends, and possible solutions.

To encourage further reaction, meetings were held at the Ottawa office of the Institute on June 25 and 26, 1985. The overall purpose of the meetings was to provide a forum for a cross-section of representatives within the social policy network to examine collectively the Discussion Paper, and to develop group reaction and direction. The agenda was based upon the themes highlighted by the individual responses to the Discussion Paper.

Fifteen people, representative of planning councils, interest groups, service organizations, business, labour, research groups, religious organizations, professional associations and professional schools (using the typology of NGO players described in the Discussion Paper), met all day on June 25th to explore social policy development from a non-government perspective. They were joined on June 26th by six government officials to explore the NGO/government interface in social policy development. The summary of individual reactions and the notes from the Social Policy meetings have been integrated into the following text to form an overall summary of reactions to the Discussion Paper.

The Social Policy Process

To reflect the changing dynamics of policy development and the process of governing, and in reaction to the Discussion Paper, the following themes have been highlighted:

Integration of Economic and Social Policy

The need to integrate social and economic policy permeated the thinking and orientation of most discussions on the development of general policy. A redefinition of issues in terms of both social and economic goals is required, along with many different fora to bring economic and social resources together. This approach challenges the "mind-set" behind earlier studies of the social policy process in Canada, and it encourages both social and economic players to become socio-economic players when advocating broad policy changes.

The Term "NGO"

The Term "NGO", an abbreviation for non-government organization, is seen as a negative way of describing non-government structures and groups because it denotes an identity in society only in terms of government. Terms used in other countries to describe all or some of the non-government sector are "the third force" and "the independent sector". The Discussion Paper used the term NGO literally, in the broad sense of referring to all sectors and groupings other than government.

Social Policy and Social Change

There is a difference in goals and in process between the development of social policy and the development of social change. Social policy seems more directly related to government agendas and action whereas social change relates more to social forces or movements in society (most often originating outside government) which seek to influence government policy. Many NGOs view themselves as players in the development of both policy and change, yet some, due to limited mandates and resources, just choose to focus either on public education and social change or on the development of social policy as defined by government-initiated agendas and consultation processes.

Values

Values, over and beyond the objective analysis of issues, play a major role in how governments and non-government groups act and make policy choices. This includes perceptions, intuition, and "visions for the future", as different sectors of society struggle to define the nature of community good. Thus, one cannot assume that social policy development results entirely from rational, objective analysis and debate.

Broad Public Support in the Most Influential Element in the Development of Social Policy

To improve the social policy process, an analytical framework is required to define, study and debate social policy. Ideally, it is a framework which government and non-government bodies would agree to.

The Nature of Social Policy Today

The discussion on defining the scope and nature of social policy indicated that definitions vary for people and organizations depending on perception, experience, culture, training and area of responsibility. For example, the following definitions of social policy were suggested: "the welfare state"; "the transfer of wealth and legal rights"; "all social actions of government"; "achieved goals that are socially-oriented"; and "people living together as social beings". An inter-cultural, historical review illustrates that the public perception of social policy varies with the orientation of dominant groups. Religious organizations and charities have played a dominant role in the past. In France, the trade movement and philosophers have strong input. Recently, in Canada, social policy tends to become part of the economic/market framework.

Both government and non-government respondents seemed uncomfortable with the Discussion Paper's definition of social policy as being the federal government's social development "envelope" and noted that the Study did not follow this definition and did not include all networks, players, and processes involved with government programmes in the social envelope.

In order to develop a definition of the parameters of social policy today, there was a need to find common agreement on values, future priorities and how to define key issues as well as the need to mesh traditional economic and social thinking by taking into consideration the social implications of economic trends and the economic implications of social trends. Mutual agreement on the important problems needing societal solutions seemed more important for change and policy development than defining what issues are social, economic, environmental, etc. The nature of a modern social consensus, the perceived speed of social change, how a social benefit is measured, are central forces in determining the nature of social policy. Specific government-oriented policy that focuses on a piece of legislation or a specific programme can more easily be defined as social or otherwise.

Some participants advocated a micro, decentralized, community-based approach to policy definition using such notions as "responsibility" and "mutual help" from an individual and community perspective. This would require a "trickle-up" approach to developing policy both within NGO organizations and networks and among different levels of government and would include a trend toward defining "new visions" and broad policy beyond and outside the delineation of government departments.

It was recognized that the establishment of an NGO typology can serve the research need to understand the social policy network but the criteria for establishing sector classifications should include the ability of an NGO to influence policy-makers, an NGO's priority goals (e.g., social, economic, global), an NGO's actual behaviour in affecting policy, and the prime instruments an organization uses to enhance policy development (e.g., research, advocacy, political parties). A group's formally-stated goal and/or mandate sometimes appears in conflict with its approach to changes in policy; furthermore, groups can fulfill a wide-range of functions and fall within more than one classification. In practice, NGOs are sensitive to being labelled because a simplistic and exclusive classification system can affect how others will perceive and relate to them. Even self-classification is resisted because it can conceal complex relationships and may affect government funding and working relationships.

Several representatives emphasized that their organizations are coalitions of various sectors (e.g., business, labour, planning councils, etc.) with the prime purpose of bringing people together to address a specific need and to advocate policy change. Coalition groups, with representation from nearly every organizational type listed in the Discussion Paper, are increasing in number as local communities mobilize to meet critical social and economic change (e.g., "Visions" group in Sydney, "Mayor's Committee" in Windsor).

Distinctions should also be made between those Advisory Councils established by government to provide advice to government and those (e.g., Planning Councils) established independently to advise the public, and between local and national groups in terms of their roles and impact on national social policy. Additionally, the growing number of self-help groups should be recognized in terms of their impact on the nature of social policy. Certain organizations, such as the United Way and information-oriented coalitions, provide an important infrastructure to other groups so that they can more effectively influence policy, and Women's groups are so unique that they may justify a separate classification within the typology structure.

It was noted that in the public policy arena, service-oriented groups tend to stay away from political controversy and thus provide a safe haven for volunteers and staff who do not wish to get politically involved in policy development. At the same time, groups with a major advocacy role attract volunteers more interested in affecting social change and government policy. National, tri-level NGOs can be "pushed and pulled" when local-level members choose service over policy activities and their national offices focus more on public education and government advocacy.

When defining and classifying sub-sectors within the social policy process, there is a difference between "power groups" and "special interest groups". There is a wide range of special interest groups trying to effect different social policies yet, at any one time, certain groups or coalitions become the power groups in terms of influencing broad policy choices. Seniors and the Women's movement are examples of current power groups seeking to influence the direction of policy.

Networking and Coalitions

Networking is viewed as an essential and on-going element in both social change and the development of policy requiring support systems that provide common information, meeting places, and a conceptual base from which action can be initiated. The elements of productive networking include a common interest, an attitude that all players have something valuable to contribute, and a setting that allows for human relationships as well as business exchanges. Workplaces, voluntary and professional organizations, and smaller, geographical communities are examples of natural settings. It is easier to have meaningful networks to enhance policy development if governments encourage such linkages and do not penalize or try to control them.

Networking can be a major force in linking the social and economic solitudes. Fora and on-going communication linkages are required in order that people with different perspectives can build trust and respect in an informal, learning atmosphere. For example, the Canadian Hospital Association and the Conference Board annually host a small meeting where a range of sectoral representatives can each bring forth for discussion their planning concerns in the health field.

Networks provide the channels for information-sharing and the building of relationships, whereas coalitions can structure relationships and commitments into more task-oriented activities. Even though coalitions are increasingly valued as a necessary step to influence policy, they can be difficult to form among socially-concerned groups because of limited resources. Few organizations have mandates or funding arrangements that enable them to delegate staffing and/or volunteer time to other structures. Coalitions could be more effective in educating the public on key themes but some policy-oriented groups are struggling financially.

Short-term coalitions with specific policy objectives seem the most effective whereas coalitions of a long-term duration must redefine periodically their goals and strategies in order to remain relevant. Sweden and France have formal, government-recognized coalition structures (e.g., Work Councils) where power is diffused and many people are encouraged to be involved. Some recent coalitions, such as the Social Policy Reform Group, are responding to a Canadian government agenda and direct their research and lobbying to government policy initiatives, whereas other broadly-based coalitions direct their attention to creating social change over time. Community coalitions can provide opportunities for citizens to influence policy and programme implementation, but they need structural models and effective ways in which to link with other communities and with the national scene.

Some fears were expressed about the potential negative effects of coalitions on policy development. On the one hand, bureaucrats and politicians can reduce contacts by working with a few coalitions rather than a large number of disconnected groups: on the other hand, coalitions may not actually represent the sectors they claim to represent and then government officials must search out other groups or depend more heavily on public polling results.

Networking and informal liaison among NGOs and government officials are valuable in lessening misconceptions and in improving working relationships. Bureaucrats are often under pressure to keep a distance and appear neutral with NGOs when on official business, yet they are free to share ideas and knowledge and, hence, build trusting relationships when invited to join non-government groups, informally. Social policy advocates within government need to have informal links with non-government social movements.

Interface of NGOs and Governments

There seemed to be general agreement that the NGO/government interface is still in great flux, with a variety of consultation approaches being used and tried, and with leaders both within and outside government suggesting the need to improve present approaches. The new Conservative federal government has advocated public consultation and "consensus-building", and consultative mechanisms have varied from the open, parliamentary debate on child benefits to selective Ministerial discussions on housing. The Nielson Task Force review of government programmes is also non-parliamentary, internal in substance, but with selective private-sector involvement. Even though the May 1985 Budget established social policy trends and expenditures, the federal consultative processes and the short list of key "influencers" appear to remain fluid with no established pattern as yet. NGOs now need to establish criteria and methods to assess their effectiveness in government consultations and this ties in closely with each group having clear objectives when participating in a range of formal and informal government relationships.

Government officials stressed the need for both informal and formal advice from NGOs and the use of many routes, both bureaucratic and political, to communicate their ideas. Informal networking was believed to carry greater influence since success often depends on personalities. At present, bureaucrats "need creative suggestions on how to do more with less", since their overriding mandate is to plan within restraints and to try to improve existing programmes. Practical suggestions from NGOs on how to improve existing services would be welcomed and would improve NGO/government relationships.

NGOs sensed pressure to accept government "pro-restraint" assumptions and values before being able to influence planning but several officials argued that NGOs in the social policy network must stress their own social values with politicians in order to provide a balanced perspective on national issues. In other words, groups should reflect their true values when meeting with politicians, rather than stating only what they believe politicians want to hear.

NGOs pointed out that they do not have the resources to consult with a wide range of government officials, but rather they need specified consultation channels that are open and effective. NGOs are looking to governments to negotiate ongoing consultation processes and to advise NGOs to deal with key emerging socio-economic issues that straddle government departments. There is increasing polarization between line departments and central spending agencies, with the central agencies making most of the major decisions on social policy spending while line departments still conduct most of the public discussions on social issues.

To change and improve the process of consultation requires a re-examination of the role of the state and the role of citizens in the policy-formulation process. There were suggestions to decentralize consultation on an ongoing basis to facilitate the building of trust and working relationships over time. The occasional national conference with no ongoing, meaningful follow-up has little long-term impact and task force studies, where the talking and the listening is often one way, have limited impact in final government decision-making. However, a change in the balance of power is under way:

- as a greater range of players chooses to become involved in social policy questions;
- as the media and research results play a greater role;
- as more voluntary organizations view policy advocacy and public education as important tasks;
- as legal and new constitutional arrangements impact on the choice of approaches available. There is increased support for governments to delegate their administrative roles in implementing social programmes, while still keeping most funding, legislative and regulative responsibilities.

Some NGO representatives felt obligated to respond to formal consultation initiated by government in order to maintain relationships, even when they questioned the value of the time and money spent, and it was observed that certain NGOs participate in government consultation (e.g., task force hearings) more to educate other publics about their perspectives on issues rather than in expectation of influencing the host government.

It was noted that most key decisions on social policy occur in federal-provincial negotiations. NGO/federal and NGO/provincial consultations are sometimes preliminary to another set of discussions and analysis that involve only officials and/or cabinet ministers, and of which the non-government sector has little knowledge. Federal-provincial negotiations on social policy inevitably include such factors as intergovernmental relations and trade-offs and government priorities may hold greater weight than the issues of funding needs and service delivery expressed by the NGOs. Thus, the determination of social policy is viewed as "closed, behind-the-door", with NGOs and the public never knowing the trade-offs nor why certain decisions are made. Examples were mentioned to illustrate this pattern of social policy development. The research, dialogue and reporting of the Pension and Fiscal-Arrangements Federal Task Forces appeared to have a limited impact on policy decisions. The present study and debate on the topic of "employable people on welfare" is taking place primarily among a few government officials with no public input. Also, the present CAP review by the Nielson Task Force involves little or no public discussion and NGO input, yet any changes in CAP could greatly affect income security and the delivery of social services.

It is further recognized that not all provinces are equal in federal-provincial discussions. and that they vary greatly in the degree of centralized service, in the matter of private-versus-public delivery, and in the level of community input. Provinces also vary in the amount of social reporting and in the withholding of statistics to such a degree that NGOs can rarely collect a complete, national picture of service delivery or social well-being.

NGO representatives asked that federal-provincial committees be more open to the public, that upcoming agendas be publicly disclosed, and that federal and provincial structures include direct NGO input. In turn, government officials asked that NGOs "stop playing one level of government against the other", that they "enable and facilitate" federal-provincial co-operation, and that informed public opinion pull federal and provincial thinking together.

Since many Canadians continue to support national standards and equity for social programmes, albeit with a diversity of services to respond to local needs, distinct yet interlocking roles for federal, provincial and local governments will continue to exist. A suggested role for NGOs is to host ongoing fora where many NGO representatives and government officials at different levels can come together for discussion and exchange of information. Such independent and somewhat neutral bodies, especially if they earn recognition and respect from different levels of government, could provide a public alternative to present federal-provincial discussions and become a step towards more direct NGO involvement in federal-provincial negotiations.

Participation, Research, Funding

Funding sources, as well as the size of budgets, affect the nature and role of NGO participation in public policy development. Potential conflict continues to exist for many voluntary organizations dependent on government funding and support, when they try to influence the policy and programme choices of government. It was noted that the business and labour players within the social policy process are in the preferred position of financial independence to facilitate research and advocacy.

The growing privatization of social services has a direct effect on how those voluntary organizations and businesses contracted to provide service will influence social policy in the future and there is a growing fear that contracting agencies will feel restricted when speaking on government-oriented issues, either publicly or privately.

Local United Ways, when allocating local volunteer dollars, also hold some control over the nature of advocacy and there is increasing pressure for local community coalitions to find independent funding in order to carry out the necessary research, information collection and public education.

There was agreement that high quality research is important to the development of social policy, not only for responsible and articulate lobbying, but also to inform the media and the public about the issues and possible solutions. In most areas of social policy, sufficient primary data are being collected in one form or another. The challenge to NGOs and to the public at large is locating this information, getting access, knowing how to use it "creatively", and in having the necessary resources to do so. More secondary, interpretative research is also required, in order to substantiate philosophical stands and policy recommendations. Researching the relationships between fields of data (e.g., social and economic) in order to obtain a more comprehensive approach to issues is probably today's greatest research gap in policy development. The meshing of concepts and traditional research frameworks is important when addressing such key policy areas as employment, child care, modern family needs, etc.

Studies in the US have shown that research has little direct impact on policy, but indirectly it frames issues and casts light on various options. In Europe there are more social scientists involved in all areas of research in contrast to the North American domination by economists and economic analysis. Thus, the social policy challenge requires more research, primarily from the NGO sector, to produce integrative, imaginary, proactive and self-critical analysis.

Generally speaking, governments at all levels should be primarily responsible for basic social statistics, for measuring overall social well-being, and for producing primary social research. In turn, NGOs should have greater access to government data, without discrimination due to lack of funds or informal contacts. Government statistics should provide the commonly-held statistical base from which there could be wide and varying interpretations. Government officials pointed out the importance of balanced, well researched and documented material when trying to influence public policy. Whereas governments should increase monthly social reporting on trends in national and local social well-being, NGOs should exercise responsibility for interpretive analysis and social commentary. In time, this could produce a more balanced, socio-economic perspective of societal trends, adjustments, and overall well-being.

More research was recommended in the area of programme evaluation with governments evaluating publicly-funded programmes but NGOs being funded to carry out independent evaluations. With the increased privatization of social and health services, public regulation of service must assure that private groups are giving high-quality, efficient services within public standards. Those NGOs dependent on government funding and closely involved in government programmes could feel "at risk" in conducting evaluations of government-related programmes.

Governments must supply comprehensive information on the nation's social well-being and its social programmes and work co-operatively to make these findings easily accessible and comprehensible. Some provinces share statistics and accounting analyses with the federal government, yet do not release them publicly, and as the federal government is not prepared to release confidential, provincial information, the data base available to the public remains incomplete. National fora were suggested as one solution to this problem in the hope that unanswered questions, identified as clearly within the public domain, would put pressure on different levels of government to share their internal statistics and findings.

Regular, ongoing social reporting by governments and research institutes, in conjunction with existing economic reporting of GNP, unemployment statistics, etc. is viewed as essential public information. Monthly or quarterly "social well-being" statistics would help to shift the present public orientation from a strictly economic framework to a more comprehensive, integrated socio-economic understanding. The social aspects of public policy could then gain equivalent value within a new socio-economic framework for policy development. Regular social reporting would also allow the policy players to reflect upon commonly-held data and to advocate policy stands within a widely understood, socio-economic framework.

There is a role for NGOs to be "interpreters" of social and economic statistics and to be "negotiating bodies" for different sets of public values. At the local community level, citizens are seeking a broader range of options for defining issues and for determining new solutions and there is increasing pressure on social policy players to provide social scenarios using publicly-available research, that includes economic as well as social data.

As modern technology encourages the use of polls and other direct public participation in policy choices, NGOs will need to increase their orientation to public education and debate. Some officials and politicians reinforce this trend when they mention that "polls reflect objectively overall public choices, whereas one is never certain just who or how many people a special interest group actually represents".

Since "policy by polls" shifts public participation more to the individual, NGOs recognized the need to develop media skills in order to be a credible part of the process. To gain initial media attention, NGOs may need to link their human and social values to economic thinking and develop partnerships with larger, like-minded institutions and organizations which already have prominent and frequent media coverage.

The information age, with sophisticated communication technology and strategies will help to determine which NGOs are sector spokesmen and hold the greatest influence over public perceptions and government action. The competition among sectors to influence public opinion is increasing, in response to the public need for information to respond to public issues. Local community resource centres may be required to provide both information and fora for mutual learning.

Future Action in Policy Development

The IRPP's preliminary exploration of the social policy process has encouraged a number of social policy players to suggest changes to existing attitudes and practices in order to enhance the development of social policy. Participants at the June social policy meeting, along with respondents to the Discussion Paper, recommended new approaches and described some models which should be used more widely. There was a belief that the roles in developing social policy for both governments and the NGO sectors will change and that the NGO/government interface must improve.

Emerging trends in the social policy field were noted as well as structural changes in the policy process and the requirement for a coming together of social and economic players towards the development of integrated socio-economic policy. In addition to those outlined in the final sections of the Discussion Paper*, the following observations and suggestions for future activities were emphasized:

* In recent years, the business community has increased its role and influence in the development of social policy by speaking out independently on broad social issues and by participating in the management of human services. Federal and provincial governments are calling for their advice, as key social policy concerns are addressed in economic and management terms. It was noted, however, that the strong business umbrella associations (e.g., Business Council on National Issues, Canadian Federation of Independent Business, and the Canadian Chamber of Commerce) do not necessarily represent the total diversity of business concerns.

* Socially-oriented groups are also becoming more involved in broad economic issues and this is occurring around public policy themes that are increasingly viewed by the public as having both economic and social consequences (e.g., employment, affordable housing, small-town industrial changes).

* Socio-economic policy needs to integrate macro and micro planning initiatives. Local communities provide valuable data, programme evaluation and information about unmet needs that need to be embodied in macro policy formulation. At the same time, national analysis of global conditions, external pressures, and directions for the country, are pertinent subjects for local debate. The coming together of local and national information is required at each point on a continuum of local/provincial/national decision-making.

* Both NGOs and governments are relating to the Charter of Rights and other "rights" legislation in order to affect social change and some of this is being done outside the legal and formal legislative structures so as to project attitudinal change towards greater equity and social justice. The use of court rulings to formalize rights has just begun.

* As society moves from a public-service monopoly for many human services to a private-public mix, the players wishing to influence social policy will

---

* Pages 31 of Part I of this document

change as will the role of the state in regard to public standards and regulations. Further study and more public discussion are required before major changes are made in this area.

- There was strong support for ongoing consultative processes of a multi-partite nature, to address both broad socio-economic policy and social programmes. The preferred model stressed equal participation of voluntary groups, business, labour, and government, with appropriate balance between men and women, and language and cultural groupings. Different structures may be required when addressing broad, socio-economic themes as opposed to specific social policy concerns (e.g., urban housing), but in either case, such structures should have:

  - an ongoing role and mandate;
  - a thematic mandate which is focussed, explainable and subject to periodic review and update;
  - participants viewed as equals;
  - smaller, more frequent meetings, rather than large, one-time conferences;
  - well-researched preparatory work and agendas;
  - opportunity for participants to add to the agenda and identify new topics for further review;
  - meetings that bring together a range of players of similar levels of responsibility and decision-making in order that problem-solving and reconciliations among equals might be achieved;
  - fora that bring together differing values and perspectives, and meetings with representation by staff specialists and lay volunteers;
  - ability to gather and distribute key information and provide media commentary and other public education.

- It is important for groups to initiate independently their own topics and research as well as addressing government agendas. For example, the Canadian Hospital Association holds joint meetings with business-oriented organizations to share information and build support for issues; and the Economic Council of Canada continues to provide an economic focus on public issues whilst recognizing the need for other research bodies (e.g., the Institute for Research on Public Policy) to help integrate both social and economic perspectives when addressing public policy. The Economic Council specifically seeks partnership arrangements with other sectors when hosting meetings on specific themes.

- Some public policy issues or "problem areas" needing immediate study and public debate were identified as follows:

  - the relationship between social welfare, unemployment insurance and employment income;
  - privatization trends and impacts;
  - analysis of the Report of the Macdonald Commission, particularly in terms of social policy;

- the impact of proposed changes on social and economic conditions; and
- the future of work and employment.

In addition, ongoing research and monitoring of the social policy process is required, including particular focussing on specific process issues such as:

- techniques of social reporting;
- role of coalitions;
- NGO involvement in federal-provincial meetings; etcetera.

- There is a particular need to mobilize resources and initiate the compilation of monthly, ongoing reporting of key social statistics and of the status of social well-being throughout Canada. Health and Welfare Canada, the Department of Finance, and Statistics Canada could collaborate in producing such monthly statements and specified NGOs could be responsible for analysis and public commentary to put the monthly statistics into context. There was also a need for governments to package social data in simulation models so as to provide for public access and to enable groups to perform their own analysis.

- Staff rotations between government and non-government groups should be increased. Since NGOs deal more directly with people and bureaucrats deal more directly with information and analysis, key players in both arenas could benefit from a mix in experience, approach and philosophy.

Conclusion

The observations and suggestions about required changes to the policy process require attitudinal and structural adjustments on the part of all existing and emerging players. Specific initiatives to provide ongoing research and discussion could come from those institutions which are national, independent and policy-oriented.

Public education and social reporting require the combined resources of central agency data banks and NGO interpretive commentary, and the increased involvement of local groups and communities in national policy making requires public policy processes that enhance meaningful involvement and shared responsibility. The list of "change agents" could vary for each recommendation, yet it is the combined commitment of players concerned with social policy that must take responsibility for initiating change and coordinating the human resources to do so.

The social policy process can evolve successfully given: an increased awareness of the existing processes; an appreciation that social agreements among Canadians will continue to change; and a common belief that future solutions to enhance the overall well-being of Canadians can be defined and implemented.

BACKGROUND NOTE

IRPP STUDY OF THE SOCIAL POLICY PROCESS

Introduction

This note attempts to set out in abbreviated form the background and rationale for a preliminary study of the social policy network, and social policy analysis and development in Canada, currently being undertaken by the Institute for Research on Public Policy (IRPP).

The process through which policy is developed, implemented and appraised, whatever the "policy sector" might be -- economic, social, environmental, cultural, defence, etc. -- involves the interplay of many participants and interests. One might refer to the cast of players which are active in any particular policy sector as a "network" or "community" (dynamic rather than static) within which there are significantly different roles and degrees of influence. Varying degrees of discipline and coherence are imposed on this process as individual concerns are aggregated, and competing interests and claims articulated and reconciled.

In the social policy area there is a host of agencies that provide representation and advocacy on behalf of particular client groups -- typically those groups within society which are less powerful or self-sufficient such as the poor, the physically and mentally handicapped, the ethnic minorities, the unemployed, the aged, the young, etc. There are also associations of experts, professionals or practitioners who provide services to these client groups, and there are the social service delivery agencies themselves. A somewhat different category is represented by those groups which contribute to policy formation and analysis from a supposedly more disinterested or comprehensive perspective -- institutes, universities, agencies, commissions, and analytic groups both inside and outside the bureaucratic or parliamentary structures, which are engaged in research, analysis and commentary related to social policy and programs.

Concerns about Effectiveness

It is clear that this loosely defined social policy community exists, and in some obvious sense "works" insofar as it provides the consultative process through which government moves forward initiatives designed to favour social development, provide essential social programs and minimize the social costs of change and economic adjustment.

It is less clear that the network is promoting effective and informed debate on social policy issues to the same extent and degree of sophistication that is occurring in other sectors. The effectiveness of political representation, lobbying, advocacy, research, analysis and commentary is crucial for the mobilization of resources to initiate or sustain social programs. Questions about the functions and modus operandi of groups which are active in policy formation, about their links to government, to constituencies or clienteles and to other members of the social policy network can thus provide a basis for understanding the present system and for assessing its overall effectiveness.

The Present Context

The need for a study of the social policy process, and of the population of organizations which are involved in it, is accentuated by a number of factors arising out of the present socio-economic context. Most important of these is the contemporary preoccupation with restraint in government spending. This concern is manifested in a number of developments -- for example, it is perceived by some that the current interest in "voluntarism" is a strategy for drawing back from government funded provision of social services; as may be the case also with the recent suggestion for reducing tax expenditures by removing the tax-exempt status of charitable organizations engaged in political advocacy. This latter issue underlines the obvious hesitancy and ambiguity that exist with respect to the appropriate role of government in funding (either explicitly or implicitly) special interest groups in the social policy area. Political and intergovernmental issues also have implications for the effectiveness of the social policy consultation process. The politically sensitive climate of federal/provincial relations combined with the diffuse and decentralized nature of both federal and provincial social service departments have posed serious dilemmas for social program delivery agencies and social policy advocacy groups. Although there is access at many different points in the policy process, there is also the possibility of confusion and duplication. For maximum impact, organizations may find it necessary to allocate limited energy and resources betwen two -- or, indeed, three -- orders of government, and there is the possibility that adequate representation of less well organized and poorer segments of the population may not occur. In addition, interest groups may tend to focus sharply on one category of needs or reforms, not only for visibility but also in order to qualify for specific government grants. Narrow definitions of problems may lead in turn to overly specialized "solutions" and result in a series of fragmented and uncoordinated government structures and programs. A different but related concern is the apparent continuing unease on the part of governments with respect to the current mix of delegated responsibilities for various social services. It is interesting in this context to note the absence of any federal regional coordinators of social development playing a role parallel to that of the Federal Economic Development Coordinators. This may be a reflection of the relative importance currently accorded to social policy vis-a-vis economic policy. Economic policy is supported by a high level of inter-departmental, intergovernmental and private sector analysis and consultation. The study of economic issues is carried out by think tanks and research institutes, some of which rely on funding from government while others are privately funded, and their work is incorporated into the economic policy development process. Examples include the authoritative empirical research and analysis carried out by such organizations as The Economic Council of Canada, The Howe Research Institute, The Conference Board of Canada, etc. In contrast, social policy research has been visible mainly in the context of Royal Commissions, and in preparations for federal/provincial conferences at both the Ministerial and official level, and for parliamentary committees and task forces. The influence of prominent research and policy organizations such as The Canada Council on Social Development and The National Welfare Council is less well known, as are the communication and consultation links between government and groups with similar goals. Some of the apparent differences in the processes of policy formation between the two sectors may be attributable to structural differences. Economic policy formation draws representations from interest groups and coalitions acting in their own self interest as economic agents. The underlying drive to influence economic policy towards general business objectives or specific sectoral or firm objectives is the primary motivation for contributing to the general debate on economic policy, and financing this effort from own revenues is seen to make eminent sense. Moreover research and commentary on economic issues can appeal to a well-developed -- even though not universally accepted -- body of macroeconomic theory and general principles of market mechanisms. In the social policy sector, by contrast, interest groups are generally created for, rather than by, a clientele, and exert their influence through weight of numbers of people rather than market position or economic clout. There is no underlying macrotheory or body of persuasive abstract principles to provide a common language in which research, commentary and debate can be carried on. Whatever the explanation for the imbalance in the level of applied analysis between the social policy sector and other policy sectors, the implications are not trivial. The danger exists that social policy concerns could be overwhelmed by the obsession with narrow indicators of international competitiveness and productive efficiency, leading to real deprivation for those less fortunate or powerful groups that are presently supported (whether adequately or not) by the social welfare net.

Rationale

The study being undertaken by the Institute for Research on Public Policy will attempt to delineate in more detail the membership and activities of what has been referred to above as the "social policy network". From the inventory of organizations which are involved in policy formation and analysis, a classification or typology will be developed in order to identify the functions which are being performed and to explore the ways in which governments might appropriately relate to different types of organization and promote their effectiveness as participants in the policy debate. The study will involve contact with representatives of key organizations and agencies, both within governments and outside. Their first-hand impressions of how, and with whom, consultation takes place will then lead into a more complete review of the most influential groups, and willl open up the fundamental questions of how social policy analysis and advocacy can be coordinated and strengthened, and of what options are available to governments for assisting in achieving this objective.

31 May 1984

NB: Copies of this Background Note were distributed to all recipients of the Questionnaire at the outset of the IRPP study in the Summer of 1984.

THE TYPOLOGY

The Classification System*

The literature on NGOs contains a number of organizational typologies. (See, for example, Secretary of State Social Trends Analysis Directorate's: The Development of a Typology of the Voluntary Sector in Canada, or other studies cited in the bibliography.) However, the bases employed in these classification systems appear to be inappropriate for a study of the social policy process. Most

---

*In building this typology, it was found that explicit common-usage vocabulary is difficult to find in either of the official languages. The vocabulary problems encountered in both languages were an overlap of the meaning of terms and, conversely, the same term having multiple meanings. These problems suggested two possible options: (1) to develop a specialized typology using an artificially created set of codes which we designed, or (2) to employ commonly-used labels for organizational types and to simultaneously collect the information required by the study as well as the background information needed to verify the respondent's classification of the ʌorganization. As it was felt that the introduction of a novel system of classifying organizations in the questionnaire would confuse respondents, it was decided to go with the second option -- to employ common-usage organizational labels.

There are a number of potential pitfalls in using such a technique. Classes may be missed in the listing provided. Respondents, finding no acceptable category, may feel forced to select a category which is somewhat inappropriate. Also, the terms may not be understood by the respondents for the reasons given above. Finally, the extra questions required for classification verification increase the bulk of the questionnaire and may reduce the response rate.

typologies were based on clientele, interest topic, or purpose of output. The basis needed for classification in this study is the organization's orientation to and involvement with social policy development. To our knowledge, the classification system described herein is the only one built on this basis.

While the study is likely to have suffered from a number of methodological problems*, the responses received have face validity and are largely in agreement with both the information collected from interviewees and the reported results from studies with similar foci.

The classes used in the questionnaire were developed through examination of the literature. Quite simply, the categories offered were those most commonly referred to in connection with social policy, structured to reduce possible areas of functional overlap so far as possible. These were:

* Advisory/Planning Councils
* Interest Groups
* Professional Associations
* Religious Organizations
* Service Organizations
* Business
* Labour Organizations
* Professional Schools
* Research Institutes

This list excludes NGOs created for purposes having no social policy impact such as promoting hobbies, the arts, recreational sports, etc. and those engaged in purely social, scientific, religious, or cultural activities. Unless an interest in social policy could be clearly identified, these categories were not entered in our listing.

In order to overcome the potential non-selection problems posed by having fixed categories, an "other" category was added. Approximately 11 percent of respondents chose this category. After examining these responses, two new categories were established: "Federal Funding Agencies" and "Non-Profit Funding Agencies". The remaining "other" respondents were found to be classifiable under either "service" or "interest". The main difficulty these respondents appeared to experience in selecting a single category lay in the fact that their organizations were performing both service and interest group activities and both of these types of activity were important to their mandate.* The choice of category in which to classify these organizations was made by the coders after taking into consideration the entirety of the questionnaire and the written material supplied by the organization. The main criterion used was the organization's overall orientation towards its benefit population rather than the membership or government. An orientation towards the benefit population was considered indicative of a service group.

As 89 percent of the organizations had little difficulty in classifying themselves, the typology appears to have been understood by and found applicable to the NGO field. Discriminant analysis showed that 55 percent of the organizations classified by the typology fitted best in the category selected.

---

* This difficulty is discussed below under Interest Groups and in Appendix C.

Given the existence of eleven categories, a random classification would have achieved a prediction rate of only 9 percent. Thus there is both methodological and statistical support for using the categories identified.

Three of the eleven categories had too few respondents to allow analysis of the results. These were non-profit funding agencies, federal funding agencies and religious organizations. As a consequence, in what follows, reference will be made to only the remaining eight organizational types.

Characterizing Organizational Types

The range of responses to most questions overlapped considerably from one organizational type to the next. However, using a four factor analysis leads to the identification of distinctive and characteristic patterns for each type of organization. The four factors were:

- sources of revenue;
- orientation to either government policy, providing services to a benefit population, or providing services to members;
- perceived impact of using information dissemination to influence social policy; and
- the size of the annual budget.

Using these four factors we can create Table 2.1.

Aspects of NGOs Common to All Types

There are several observations based on the questionnaire which are general in nature and show little variance between categories of NGO in this typology. One such observation is that there is a general propensity for all of the selected types of NGO organizations to strive to influence government policy. Only eight percent of the respondents stated that they did not try to influence social policy. Except for one respondent in the interest group, these negative responses were all in the Service, Research, and Professional Schools categories.

Another general observation relates to the size of NGOs. In each of the NGO categories it was noted that there was at least one very large organization in terms of professional staff. Within their class, these large organizations had at least twice the number of professionals on staff as compared to the next largest organization. Such a discontinuity may, in part, be explained by the next general observation.

The catalogues which identify those Canadian NGOs which are not of a purely local nature contain approximately 9,000 main entries. It is estimated that one-third to one-half of these would be participants in the social policy field at one level or another. The very size of this sub-field suggests the probable

Table 2.1

Four Factor Analysis of Organizational Types[1]

Organizational type	organization is primarily oriented towards [2]	perceives information dissemination as most effective means of influencing policy [3]	major source of revenue [4]	size of budget [5]
Advisory/Plan	Gov't Policy	No	Government	Medium
Business	Members	No	Non-Gov't	Medium
Interest	Gov't Policy	Yes	Government	Small
Labour	Members	Yes	Non-Gov't	Large
Prof. Assoc.	Members	Yes	Non-Gov't	Small
Prof. School	Benefit Pop.	No	Government	Small
Research Inst.	Gov't Policy	No	Government	Small
Service	Benefit Pop.	No	Government	Large

Notes:

(1)   Table is constructed from aggregated unweighted numerical responses.

(2)   Orientation determined on basis of respondents' ranking of organizational purposes. Only three purposes of the six possible were selected for this table, the others being research, education of the general public and education of professionals.

(3)   Perception based on aggregated responses on five point scale of effectiveness of types of activity in influencing social policy. Aggregated scores for each activity were then ranked within each class. Within the ranking of the six activities, information dissemination was found either at the top or the bottom.

(4)   The percentage of revenue from specific sources relative to the total was compared and the largest relative source identified.

(5)   Small is equal or less than $999,000 on average.
Medium is $1 million to $2.9 million on average.
Large is greater than $3 million on average.

existence of a number of common organizational and interactional problems ranging from sharing data, organization and co-ordination around specific issues, and communicating information. One would expect a set of larger NGOs to emerge and rationalize the diversity. Given the observation above, this may be what is happening. If so, then either the process is slow or is stalled. The study indicates that a surge in new NGOs occurred between 1971 and 1976. Twenty-five percent of all responding NGOs came into existence during this six year period. Thus there have been at least ten years in which amalgamation could have occurred yet evidently it has not. As the waste of time and money in administrative overlap must be substantial, the continued unorganized diversity suggests that some organizational component must be missing. Three reasons which might account for the non-rationalized state of the NGO field are:

(i) a wide diversity of NGO interests with little or no overlap,
(ii) a lack of incentive or the existence of a disincentive which affects the NGOs and therefore prevents the creation of an overarching co-ordinating body, and
(iii) the current existence of a network which efficiently resolves most of these problems and decreases the value of more formal associations.

The questionnaire results and interviews suggest that the interests of the various NGOs are not, in fact, so divergent. Therefore, on the face of it, there would seem to be strong incentives for NGOs to work closely with each other. Further, no major disincentive appears to block formal association or mergers. This failure to find support for possibilities (i) and (ii) suggest that the third reason may be more correct.

In examining the possibility of an existing network, it was first noted that the majority of NGOs are small, tend to be built around individuals, and initially have specific, not general interests. It is the personal dedication, time, energy, ability, and charisma of the leading figure in the smaller NGOs that binds the organization together. Should the organization, while still nascent, lose this individual its demise often follows. A second point to be noted is the advantage a small, independent NGO has over a branch office arrangement. The small independent can operate freely in its specific environment and can take advantage of localized opportunites. In contrast, Branch offices may be constrained by national policies developed at Head Office and these policies may not allow the flexibility needed to produce results most efficiently. The increased efficiency of the small independent NGO, together with the independent and entrepreneurial nature of their leading figures, suggest that they may not view functioning as a branch of a larger NGO as an advantage . They may fiercely defend their independence and be completely unwilling to merge with either a national or provincial organization.

However, working in isolation does have its costs and most of these are related to decreased flows of information. Notice of grant opportunities may be missed, along with offers of shared resources, communications, and publicity. Such losses may or may not outweigh the efficiency gains mentioned above. In either case, however, the solution is the same: to get plugged into a communication network.

In part, this solution may be found at specialized NGO conferences and fora. While these meetings cannot provide all of the information needed by NGOs, they can provide the opportunities needed to develop the interpersonal contacts necessary to create an informal communication network. The existence of such a network is suggested in several interviews and would help to explain why the survey did not find a strong formal network. Instead of a formal network, the NGOs may operate an extensive interpersonal and informal network. If so, then on a formal level, we would expect to see only loose federations, ad hoc task forces and short-term coalitions. This is, in fact, what we do see.

Perhaps as an extension of this inter-personal networking is the belief, common amongst NGOs, that informal liaison with government is the most effective means of influencing social policy. While the study did not closely investigate the inter-personal linkages between NGOs and both governments and the bureaucracy, other studies (See Pross, 1982) state that such linkages are inevitable whether one accepts the _Estatisme_ view where these linkages are fostered by government actors or a mechanistic systemic view which, more simply, notes constant personnel exchanges between the bureaucracy and NGOs. Inter-personal networking may explain, in part, why the study found that most NGOs were located in the capital cities appropriate to their level of policy interest.

Given the NGOs belief in the effectiveness of informal liaison, a question arises as to the techniques which NGOs actually use to influence policy. Only 26 percent mentioned activities which could be classified under informal liaison. The most frequently cited category of influencing activities was formal liaison with government. Over 50 percent of those reporting indicated engaging in this activity.

General comments on the Canadian social policy process were very divergent. No single comment was repeated by over 20 percent of those responding. Such differences in perspective reflect the divergent views and roles played by the NGOs in the social policy field. The overall sense conveyed by the comments was that there is no formal, constitutionally-defined role or structure in which NGOs can legitimately operate. Expanding on this theme, we can say that NGOs operate in a "zone" constitutionally occupied by both individuals and governments. On the one hand, individuals in Canadian society have a "moral" obligation to assist the less fortunate and, additionally, a right to make known their views and opinions. In both cases NGOs are commonly the medium used. However, individuals are free to offer or withhold their assistance, allegiance, and charity to and from whatsoever NGO they wish, and whenever they wish to do so. On the other hand. Governments have a mandate based on the welfare state philosophy and in economic rationalism to care for business, the poor, the sick and the weak, and to seek out the views of the electorate. In exercising this mandate, governments also may or may not choose to listen to, assist, or cooperate with any particular NGO. While both individuals and governments generally recognize the concerns of NGOs, and their potential as intermediaries between the governed and the governors, neither is willing to surrender to the NGOs their responsibilities or authority. Further, both individuals and government want a measure of control over the expenditures made by NGOs on their behalf. Consequently, NGOs find themselves both encouraged and constrained. They are told that they have an important societal role to play and yet, at the whim of individuals or government, they can find their contribution down-played or ignored. Individuals frequently attempt to advance their personal circumstances, conditions, or political image through contact with NGOs but once these personal goals are achieved, they withdraw their assistance and support. Similarly, NGOs often complain that consultations sponsored by the government are used to gain support or publicity for a change which is to be instituted no matter what opinions the NGOs provide. NGOs frequently view such events as Royal Commissions and public hearings as being crafted so as not to produce meaningful results. NGOs are virtually forced to join in these consultations in order to fulfill their mandate though they know in advance what the outcome will be and know also that their precious and limited resources will be strained by their involvement. It is the lack of a constitutionally defined role in the social policy process which allows NGOs to be placed in this ambiguous position.

Typology of Organizations Influential in Social Policy

Advisory/Planning Councils

Advisory/Planning Councils are oriented towards government policy. They are expressly created to attempt to influence governments and their major means of doing so is through research. They generally do not provide services to a benefit population nor are they oriented to servicing the needs of their membership. Their largest source of funding is government. The average annual budget is in the range of $1 - $1.5 million. They do not perceive information dissemination to be useful and prefer to use formal and especially informal liaison with government.

Business Associations

Business Associations were found to be self-financed groups primarily oriented to members. Serving the membership was viewed as the most important purpose of these organizations, followed by the promotion of policy or program change. These organizations have a membership with whom they consult as to which policies to advocate or influence.

Business Associations do not perceive information dissemination to be the best means of influencing government policy. They perceive the use of informal liaison with government and service delivery activities to be more effective means. However, in stating what they actually do to influence policy, business associations most frequently listed formal liaison activities, such as the submission of briefs and papers. Their average budget is in the medium-size range of $1 - $1.5 million and their major source of funds is the private sector. On a three point scale the business organizations rated the security of their core funding at 2.0.

Interest Groups

The least homogeneous classification in the typology was interest groups. While a general characterization is possible, it should be noted that there are two sub-categories within this classification.

Generally, interest groups can be characterized by their being funded largely by government, having a smaller budget ($400 - $800 thousand), and perceiving information dissemination to be the most effective means of influencing social policy. Of all classifications, interest groups rated information dissemination most highly. The least effective means of influencing social policy were perceived to be service delivery activities and formal liaison with government. Their general orientation, subject to what is indicated below, is towards government policy.

Within this classification, there are two sub-categories distinguishable on the basis of whether or not they provide services to a benefit group. As noted earlier, there appears to be a continuum between service organizations and interest groups. At the service end of the continuum are NGOs which provide services and have little interest in or involvement with social policy. At the other extreme are interest groups which have no benefit population to serve and are focussed on social policy changes. In the mid-ground are organizations which combine these two foci.

There are significant differences and similarities between these two subgroups within the interest category. In Table 2.2 are shown the standardized ranks of the various types of activities in terms of their importance to the organization's purpose. There are noticeable trends amongst the three categories. As would be expected, the importance of providing services to a benefit population decreases with involvement in interest group activities and the loss of the benefit population. The trend is interesting when compared with provision of services to members. Interest groups, whether with or without a benefit population, are significantly more involved in both the promotion of programs and policy changes and the education of the public than are service groups.

The same characteristic trend is also apparent in average percentages of time spent in service delivery, formal liaison with government, and especially information dissemination, as well as in the size of the organization's professional staff, and the percentage of funds received from government (See Table 2.3).

One scenario suggesting how this continuum might emerge over time states that service groups whose program, benefit population, or funding is threatened by changes in government policy may feel the necessity of becoming more politically active and start to voice their concerns. If the program is cut, they may still carry on but at a reduced service level with volunteer help shifted increasingly towards policy advocacy. Advocacy requires less funding than service delivery and the manpower may already be available. At some later

Table 2.2

Trends in organizational purpose between interest and service groups

Is Activity of Importance to Organization's Purpose	Service Organization	Interest Group with Benefit Population	Interest Group with No Benefit Population	Comments
Service to Benefit Pop.	1.78	0.04	-1.79	Increasing importance of benefit pop. as one is gained and interest activities decline.
Service to Members	0.09	-0.17	0.10	No significant difference between. types
Promotional Prog/policy Change	0.44	1.43	1.21	Noticeable difference between service and interest groups
Education of Public	0.22	0.87	1.03	Trend towards more education of public as interest group activities increase
Education of Professionals	-1.31	-1.04	-0.48	Education of professionals is less important when group has benefit population
Policy Research	-1.00	-1.48	-0.07	If type has benefit population, then research is less important

Note: Scores in standard deviation from the class mean. Positive score indicates that activity was of greater than average importance.

Table 2.3

Trends in Service and Interest Groups over Selected Variables

Variable	Service Organization	Interest Benefit Population	Interest No benefit Population
Percentage time - formal liaison with government	7.0	8.6	9.7
Percentage time - Service Delivery	41.2	24.7	20.4
Percentage time - Information Dissemination	9.7	16.6	22.4
Size of Professional Staff	25.8	7.8	3.7
Percentage funds from Government	55.3	42.6	29.8

point, further funding cuts may completely delete service delivery activities and the remaining organization could become fully oriented to interest group activities. The process outlined here may also be reversible with interest groups setting up services in order to either implement what they believe is right or to increase their flow of funds.

With respect to which social policy concerns were voiced and which were not, a relatively frequent comment made by members of interest groups was that their particular concerns were not given significant consideration by their interest group. However, these same members state that they would continue their support of the interest group because it was the best vehicle available to express their view-point to government. It seems that interest groups are providing a service that their members believe to be essential for success. Thus, disenchantment does not necessarily lead to a lapse in organizational support. Members seem unwilling to lose the potential value of their membership even though at any particular point in time the interest group may not be addressing their specific problems.

Labour Organizations

Labour organizations are characterized by large budgets - over $3 million on average and virtually all of this funding comes from membership dues. Perhaps it is for this reason that Labour gave the highest security of funding ratings for both core and program funding.

Labour Organizations have a strong orientation towards their members. They do not have a direct benefit population and their main interaction with government related to those concerns they believed to be important to their membership. Seventy percent of the Labour Organizations stated that service to members was the activity most important to their organizational purpose. The remaining 30 percent felt that the promotion of policy or program changes was of greatest importance.

In attempting to influence social policy, Labour Organizations felt information dissemination to be the most effective means available. They back this belief by listing information dissemination, especially the use of the media, as the activity most often engaged in to influence social policy.

Labour groups tend to have the largest staffs of all the NGOs, the average being 57.2 persons on the professional staff and 46.3 persons on the support staff.

Professional Associations

Professional associations were found to be very similar to interest groups, differing in the four factors only in that most of their income came from non-government sources. Their budgets were small ($400 - $800 thousand), and their general orientation was towards government rather than their members or a benefit population, although there was some variation in this. Most professional associations have some self-policing powers and arrange conferences on topics of interest to their members, whereas interest groups more rarely reported the provision of such services; both types believed that the use of information dissemination was an effective method of influencing social policy.

Professional Schools

Professional schools are characterized by small budgets ($400 - $800 thousand) virtually all of which comes from government. They are oriented towards providing services to a benefit population (students) and believe that information dissemination is not the best way of influencing social policy. Rather, they see informal liaison as the most effective means of policy influence, followed by the provision of service delivery activities. In reporting what they actually did to influence social policy, however, professional schools most frequently reported doing research.

It should be remembered that most professional schools exist within the confines of universities and therefore their role in policy development is commonly one step removed from the NGO/Government interactions characteristic of the other organizational types. Yet because of the influential role they play in providing ideas and showing research results to future policy analysts, these schools may have a middle-to-long term impact on social policy. Beyond the organizational aspect of social policy influence, it was reported on several occasions that there is an increasing trend amongst members of university faculties to accept research contracts for studies outside of the university. If this trend continues, universities may provide an important source of expertise for the study of social policy.

Research Institutes

Research institutes are characterized by having small budgets ($400 - $800 thousand) which come mainly from government, an orientation towards government policy, and a negative perception of the use of information dissemination to influence social policy. Most research institutes (69 percent) report they do not have a benefit population and just under half (47 percent) report no membership. This classification regards research as a more effective means of influencing policy. Performing research is the 'raison d'etre' of this class with 79 percent ranking it as either the most, or the second most important activity in achieving their organizational purpose. Relative to all other NGO classes, research institutes have the least interest in the direct promotion of policy or program change.

Service Groups

Service groups are characterized as having larger annual budgets (over $3 million); most of the funding (55 percent) comes from government. Generally, service organizations felt fairly secure about their core funding, rating it at 1.8 on a three-point scale. However, they were quite insecure with respect to their program and project funding (rating of 2.5)

Service groups are strongly oriented towards providing services to a benefit population (78 percent of Service Organizations rated this activity as the most important to their organization's purpose and backed this up by spending an average of 41.3 percent of organization time on service delivery). The next highest activity was information dissemination which used an average of 9.7 percent of reported time. This service is performed despite their acknowledgement that service delivery activities do not influence social policy.

Policy influence is perceived to come as a result of informal and formal liaison with government. Information dissemination was perceived to be the least effective means of influencing social policy.

A statistical typology of the eight organizational types is provided in the remaining pages of this Appendix.

A Statistical Typology of Eight Organizational Types

Advisory or Planning Councils

Organizational type—Advisory or Planning Council

Year established:

Average	1963
Median	1972
Range	1908 to 1984

Importance of specified activities to organization's purpose (in percent):

Activity	Most Imp.	2	3	4	5	6	N/A	Ave.
Service to benefit population	16	0	8	4	4	12	56	3.4
Service to members	8	20	8	8	20	4	32	3.4
Promotion of Prog/policy change	50	15	27	4	0	0	4	1.8
Education of public	32	4	21	21	11	4	7	2.8
Education of professionals	4	13	4	17	13	17	30	4.1
Policy research	23	31	15	15	4	0	12	2.4

Average percent of Organization time spent on selected activities:

Organization Maintenance	12
Service Delivery	12
Group Liaison	11
Informal Government Liaison	6
Formal Government Liaison	5
Social Research	19
Information Dissemination	15
Miscellaneous	20

Perceived effectiveness of activities on influencing Government social policy (percent).

Activity	Very Effec	2	Effec	4	Not Effec	DK	Not Done	Ave.
Service Delivery	7	7	19	26	4	7	30	3.2
Group Liaison	7	21	39	18	0	4	11	2.8
Informal Gov't Liaison	11	29	29	14	4	7	7	2.7
Formal Gov't Liaison	15	26	22	7	11	4	15	2.0
Social Policy Research	4	48	20	20	0	0	8	2.6
Information Dissemination	8	19	35	31	4	0	4	3.0

Percentage of Advisory/Planning Councils attempting to influence social policy = 92.9

How Advisory/Planning Councils try to influence social policy:

Activity	Percent Mention
Briefs and position papers	39
Research on social issues	35
Group liaison	35
Information dissemination	31
Education of public	27
Informal liaison with government	27
Formal liaison	23
Publications and editorials	23
Public meetings	23

Staffing (percentage in each row equals 100):

Type of Staff	Number of Employees					
	0	1-9	10-29	30-49	50-99	100+
Full time professional	8	81	8	0	4	0
Full time support	8	84	4	0	4	0
Contract workers	100	0	0	0	0	0
Casual employees	100	0	0	0	0	0
Volunteers	13	30	---35---		13	9
Total staff	0	37	---33---		11	19

Funding policy re: Federal Government:

Acceptance of funds	43
Non-acceptance of funds	0
No definite policy	57

Funding policy re: Provincial Government:

Acceptance of funds	42
Non-acceptance of funds	4
No definite policy	54

Funding policy re: Municipal Government:

Acceptance of funds	50
Non-acceptance of funds	4
No policy	46

Funding policy re: Corporate/Private Sources:

Acceptance of funds	46
Non-acceptance of funds	4
No policy	50

Funding policy re: Non-profit sources:

Acceptance of funds	39
Non-acceptance of funds	4
No policy	57

Percent of organizations receiving funds from various sources:

Source	| Amount of Funds Received (Percent)							
	0	1-10	11-25	26-50	51-75	76-99	100	Avg.
Government	17	10	7	33	0	20	13	45.4
Organization activity	33	50	13	0	3	0	3	11.4
Private sector	57	40	3	0	0	0	0	3.0
Non-profit orgs	43	10	3	17	20	7	0	26.0

Security of Core funding:

Secure	29
Fairly secure	32
Not assured	29

Security of Program/Project funding:

Secure	8
Fairly secure	38
Not assured	54

Total 1983 expenditure budget:

Under $50,000	15
$50 to $100,000	19
$101 to $300,000	31
$301 to $1 million	27
$1 to $3 million	0
$3 to $10 millin	4
over $10 million	4

Business Organizations

Organizational type—Business

Year established:

Average	1960 (outlier remove)
Median	1953
Range	1896 to 1981

Importance of specified activities to organization's purpose (in percent):

Activity	Most Imp.	2	3	4	5	6	N/A	Ave.
Service to benefit population	0	0	0	25	0	0	75	4.0
Service to members	67	17	0	17	0	0	0	1.7
Promotion of Prog/policy change	50	33	0	0	0	0	17	1.4
Education of public	0	17	50	0	0	0	33	2.8
Education of professionals	25	0	25	25	0	0	25	2.7
Policy research	20	20	20	0	20	0	20	2.8

Average percent of Organization time spent on selected activities:

Organization Maintenance	10
Service Delivery	10
Group Liaison	6
Informal Government Liaison	9
Formal Government Liaison	9
Social Research	8
Information Dissemination	12
Miscellaneous	36

Perceived effectiveness of activities on influencing Government social policy (percent).

Activity	Very Effec	2	Effec	4	Not Effec	DK	Not Done	Ave.
Service Delivery	14	71	0	0	0	14	0	1.8
Group Liaison	0	14	43	14	14	14	0	3.0
Informal Govt Liaison	29	43	14	0	0	14	0	1.8
Formal Govt Liaison	29	43	0	14	0	14	0	2.0
Social Policy Research	13	13	38	13	0	25	0	2.7
Information Dissemination	0	17	33	17	17	17	0	3.4

Percentage of Business Organizations attempting to influence social policy = 100.0

How Business Organizations try to influence social policy:

Activity	Percent Mention
Briefs and position papers	57
Formal liaison with government	57
Meet with government authorities	29
Research on social issues	29
Public meetings	29

Staffing (percentage in each row equals 100):

Type of Staff	Number of Employees					
	0	1-9	10-29	30-49	50-99	100+
Full time professional	0	83	0	17	0	0
Full time support	17	67	0	0	0	17
Contract workers	0	0	0	0	0	0
Casual employees	0	0	0	0	0	0
Volunteers	20	0	---20---		40	20
Total staff	0	14	---29---		14	43

Funding policy re: Federal Government:

Acceptance of funds	43
Non-acceptance of funds	14
No definite policy	43

Funding policy re: Provincial Government:

Acceptance of funds	40
Non-acceptance of funds	20
No definite policy	40

Funding policy re: Municipal Government:

Acceptance of funds	40
Non-acceptance of funds	20
No policy	40

Funding policy re: Corporate/Private Sources:

Acceptance of funds	83
Non-acceptance of funds	17
No policy	0

Funding policy re: Non-profit sources:

Acceptance of funds	20
Non-acceptance of funds	20
No policy	60

Percent of organizations receiving funds from various sources:

Source	Amount of Funds Received (Percent)							
	0	1-10	11-25	26-50	51-75	76-99	100	Avg.
Government	63	13	13	0	0	13	0	15.3
Organization activity	38	25	0	13	25	0	0	25.2
Private sector	38	0	0	13	13	13	25	47.0
Non-profit orgs	100	0	0	0	0	0	0	0.0

Security of Core funding:

Secure	38
Fairly secure	25
Not assured	38

Security of Program/Project funding:

Secure	0
Fairly secure	57
Not assured	43

Total 1983 expenditure budget:

Under $50,000	29
$50 to $100,000	0
$101 to $300,000	43
$301 to $1 million	14
$1 to $3 million	0
$3 to $10 millin	14
over $10 million	0

Interest Groups

Organizational type—Interest Groups

Year established:

Average	1965 (outlier remove)
Median	1972
Range	1870 to 1983

Importance of specified activities to organization's purpose (in percent):

Activity	Most Imp.	2	3	4	5	6	N/A	Ave.
Service to benefit population	18	6	6	0	3	12	56	3.0
Service to members	23	20	17	3	9	6	20	2.8
Promotion of Prog/policy change	40	28	13	13	3	0	5	2.1
Education of public	27	37	10	10	2	5	10	2.3
Education of professionals	14	11	14	17	20	3	20	3.3
Policy research	8	10	28	25	15	3	13	3.4

Average percent of Organization time spent on selected activities:

Organization Maintenance	11
Service Delivery	21
Group Liaison	11
Informal Government Liaison	9
Formal Government Liaison	9
Social Research	11
Information Dissemination	18
Miscellaneous	10

Perceived effectiveness of activities on influencing Government social policy (percent).

Activity	Very Effec	2	Effec	4	Not Effec	DK	Not Done	Ave.
Service Delivery	9	17	23	20	3	6	23	2.9
Group Liaison	5	36	41	10	3	3	3	2.7
Informal Govt Liaison	10	40	20	15	5	8	3	2.6
Formal Govt Liaison	5	33	28	20	5	5	5	2.9
Social Policy Research	8	35	43	8	0	3	3	2.5
Information Dissemination	18	38	30	10	0	5	0	2.3

Percentage of Interest Groups attempting to influence social policy = 95.5

How Interest Groups try to influence social policy:

Activity	Percent Mention
Briefs and position papers	56
Formal liaison with government	39
Group liaison	39
Public awareness through media	28
Informal liaison with government	26
Information dissemination	26
Public pressure through media	18
Research on social issues	18

Staffing (percentage in each row equals 100):

Type of Staff	Number of Employees					
	0	1-9	10-29	30-49	50-99	100+
Full time professional	13	65	13	5	0	0
Full time support	17	66	9	3	6	0
Contract workers	100	0	0	0	0	0
Casual employees	100	0	0	0	0	0
Volunteers	8	14	---43---		11	5
Total staff	0	20	---42---		20	18

Funding policy re: Federal Government:

Acceptance of funds	57
Non-acceptance of funds	0
No definite policy	42

Funding policy re: Provincial Government:

Acceptance of funds	58
Non-acceptance of funds	3
No definite policy	39

Funding policy re: Municipal Government:

Acceptance of funds	41
Non-acceptance of funds	8
No policy	51

Funding policy re: Corporate/Private Sources:

Acceptance of funds	55
Non-acceptance of funds	5
No policy	40

Funding policy re: Non-profit sources:

Acceptance of funds	55
Non-acceptance of funds	3
No policy	43

Percent of organizations receiving funds from various sources:

Source	Amount of Funds Received (Percent)							
	0	1-10	11-25	26-50	51-75	76-99	100	Avg.
Government	32	4	16	16	11	29	0	34.0
Organization activity	41	23	16	2	11	5	2	18.3
Private sector	19	34	7	7	5	2	2	12.3
Non-profit orgs	77	9	5	5	5	0	0	6.1

Security of Core funding:

Secure	31
Fairly secure	40
Not assured	29

Security of Program/Project funding:

Secure	7
Fairly secure	42
Not assured	48

Total 1983 expenditure budget:

Under $50,000	35
$50 to $100,000	13
$101 to $300,000	20
$301 to $1 million	13
$1 to $3 million	8
$3 to $10 millin	13
over $10 million	0

Labour Organizations

Organizational type—Labour Organizations

Year established:

Average	1945
Median	1955
Range	1905 to 1982

Importance of specified activities to organization's purpose (in percent):

Activity	Most Imp.	2	3	4	5	6	N/A	Ave.
Service to benefit population	0	10	0	30	10	20	30	4.6
Service to members	70	30	0	0	0	0	0	1.3
Promotion of Prog/policy change	30	20	40	0	10	0	0	2.4
Education of public	0	0	56	11	22	11	0	3.9
Education of professionals	0	10	10	20	0	10	50	3.8
Policy research	0	22	0	22	44	11	0	4.2

Average percent of Organization time spent on selected activities:

Organization Maintenance	4
Service Delivery	17
Group Liaison	5
Informal Government Liaison	8
Formal Government Liaison	14
Social Research	10
Information Dissemination	18
Miscellaneous	24

Perceived effectiveness of activities on influencing Government social policy (percent).

Activity	Very Effec	2	Effec	4	Not Effec	DK	Not Done	Ave.
Service Delivery	0	13	25	38	13	0	13	3.6
Group Liaison	0	0	50	38	0	13	0	3.4
Informal Govt Liaison	0	50	0	50	0	0	0	3.0
Formal Govt Liaison	13	13	25	50	0	0	0	3.1
Social Policy Research	0	38	38	25	0	0	0	2.9
Information Dissemination	0	50	25	25	0	0	0	2.8

Labour Organizations

Percentage of Labour Organizations attempting to influence social policy = 100.0

How Labour Organizations try to influence social policy:

Activity	Percent Mention
Information dissemination	70
Group liaison	50
Formal liaison with government	40
Group coalitions	30
Briefs and position papers	30
Research on social issues	30
Public awareness through media	30

Staffing (percentage in each row equals 100):

Type of Staff	Number of Employees					
	0	1-9	10-29	30-49	50-99	100+
Full time professional	0	60	0	10	10	20
Full time support	0	60	0	10	10	20
Contract workers	100	0	0	0	0	0
Casual employees	90	0	0	0	0	10
Volunteers	33	0	--- 0---		0	67
Total staff	0	25	---25---		0	50

Funding policy re: Federal Government:

Acceptance of funds	50
Non-acceptance of funds	0
No definite policy	50

Funding policy re: Provincial Government:

Acceptance of funds	38
Non-acceptance of funds	0
No definite policy	63.

Funding policy re: Municipal Government:

Acceptance of funds	14
Non-acceptance of funds	0
No policy	86

Funding policy re: Corporate/Private Sources:

Acceptance of funds	0
Non-acceptance of funds	14
No policy	86

Labour Organizations

Funding policy re: Non-profit sources:

Acceptance of funds	38
Non-acceptance of funds	0
No policy	63

Percent of organizations receiving funds from various sources:

	Amount of Funds Received (Percent)							
Source	0	1-10	11-25	26-50	51-75	76-99	100	Avg.
Government	70	20	0	10	0	0	0	3.5
Organization activity	60	0	0	0	10	0	30	37.0
Private sector	100	0	0	0	0	0	0	0.0
Non-profit orgs	100	0	0	0	0	0	0	0.0

Security of Core funding:

Secure	56
Fairly secure	44
Not assured	0

Security of Program/Project funding:

Secure	43
Fairly secure	43
Not assured	14

Total 1983 expenditure budget:

Under $50,000	0
$50 to $100,000	0
$101 to $300,000	0
$301 to $1 million	33
$1 to $3 million	11
$3 to $10 millin	22
over $10 million	33

Professional Associations

Organizational type—Professional Associations

Year established:

Average	1947
Median	1950
Range	1905 to 1981

Importance of specified activities to organization's purpose (in percent):

Activity	Most Imp.	2	3	4	5	6	N/A	Ave.
Service to benefit population	0	8	23	8	0	8	54	3.5
Service to members	41	29	6	24	0	0	0	2.1
Promotion of Prog/policy change	22	28	33	11	6	0	0	2.5
Education of public	0	17	22	28	28	6	0	3.8
Education of professionals	31	13	13	6	13	6	19	2.7
Policy research	0	13	19	25	19	6	19	3.8

Average percent of Organization time spent on selected activities:

Organization Maintenance	10
Service Delivery	11
Group Liaison	5
Informal Government Liaison	8
Formal Government Liaison	13
Social Research	11
Information Dissemination	20
Miscellaneous	22

Perceived effectiveness of activities on influencing Government social policy (percent).

Activity	Very Effec	2	Effec	4	Not Effec	DK	Not Done	Ave.
Service Delivery	11	6	17	6	22	22	17	3.1
Group Liaison	6	6	53	24	0	6	6	3.1
Informal Govt Liaison	21	37	11	21	0	5	5	2.4
Formal Govt Liaison	11	16	47	16	0	5	5	2.8
Social Policy Research	0	25	31	25	0	13	6	3.0
Information Dissemination	15	31	31	15	8	15	8	2.7

Professional Associations

Percentage of Professional Associations attempting to influence social policy = 100.0

How Professional Associations try to influence social policy:

Activity	Percent Mention
Formal liaison	63
Briefs and position papers	56
Information dissemination	38
Informal liaison with government	31
Group liaison	31
Research on social issues	19
Task force/study groups with follow-up	19

Staffing (percentage in each row equals 100):

Type of Staff	Number of Employees					
	0	1-9	10-29	30-49	50-99	100+
Full time professional	22	61	11	0	0	6
Full time support	22	50	6	6	11	6
Contract workers	100	0	0	0	0	0
Casual employees	100	0	0	0	0	0
Volunteers	0	7	---22---		29	43
Total staff	0	12	---24---		24	25

Funding policy re: Federal Government:

Acceptance of funds	35
Non-acceptance of funds	0
No definite policy	65

Funding policy re: Provincial Government:

Acceptance of funds	41
Non-acceptance of funds	0
No definite policy	59

Funding policy re: Municipal Government:

Acceptance of funds	31
Non-acceptance of funds	0
No policy	69

Funding policy re: Corporate/Private Sources:

Acceptance of funds	39
Non-acceptance of funds	0
No policy	61

Funding policy re: Non-profit sources:

Acceptance of funds	41
Non-acceptance of funds	0
No policy	59

Percent of organizations receiving funds from various sources:

Source	Amount of Funds Received (Percent)							
	0	1-10	11-25	26-50	51-75	76-99	100	Avg.
Government	53	16	5	11	11	0	5	17
Organization activity	21	5	11	21	5	5	32	49
Private sector	74	16	0	0	0	11	0	10
Non-profit orgs	84	11	5	0	0	0	0	2

Security of Core funding:

Secure	47
Fairly secure	47
Not assured	7

Security of Program/Project funding:

Secure	28
Fairly secure	21
Not assured	50

Total 1983 expenditure budget:

Under $50,000	33
$50 to $100,000	0
$101 to $300,000	22
$301 to $1 million	28
$1 to $3 million	6
$3 to $10 millin	11
over $10 million	0

Professional Schools

Organizational type—Professional Schools

Year established:

Average	1963 (outlier removed)
Median	1971
Range	1864 to 1975

Importance of specified activities to organization's purpose (in percent):

Activity	Most Imp.	2	3	4	5	6	N/A	Ave.
Service to benefit population	0	0	14	60	14	0	71	4.0
Service to members	29	0	0	14	0	0	57	2.0
Promotion of Prog/policy change	13	25	13	25	0	0	25	2.7
Education of public	0	11	22	11	11	0	44	2.9
Education of professionals	67	11	11	0	0	0	11	1.4
Policy research	11	44	11	0	0	0	33	2.0

Average percent of Organization time spent on selected activities:

Organization Maintenance	9
Service Delivery	15
Group Liaison	4
Informal Government Liaison	3
Formal Government Liaison	2
Social Research	25
Information Dissemination	14
Miscellaneous	28

Perceived effectiveness of activities on influencing Government social policy (percent).

Activity	Very Effec	2	Effec	4	Not Effec	DK	Not Done	Ave.
Service Delivery	0	33	50	0	0	17	0	2.6
Group Liaison	0	17	33	0	0	17	33	2.7
Informal Govt Liaison	0	50	33	0	0	17	0	2.4
Formal Govt Liaison	0	0	33	33	0	0	33	3.5
Social Policy Research	0	11	67	11	0	0	11	3.0
Information Dissemination	0	0	100	0	0	0	0	3.0

Percentage of Professional Schools attempting to influence social policy = 90.0

How Professional Schools try to influence social policy:

Activity	Percent Mention
Research on social issues	50
Service delivery activities	25
Informal liaison with government	25
Formal liaison with government	25
Information dissemination	25

Staffing (percentage in each row equals 100):

Type of Staff	Number of Employees					
	0	1-9	10-29	30-49	50-99	100+
Full time professional	0	60	30	0	10	0
Full time support	0	70	20	10	0	0
Contract workers	100	0	0	0	0	0
Casual employees	100	0	0	0	0	0
Volunteers	71	0	0	0	0	29
Total staff	0	13	---50---		13	25

Funding policy re: Federal Government:

Acceptance of funds	100
Non-acceptance of funds	0
No definite policy	0

Funding policy re: Provincial Government:

Acceptance of funds	100
Non-acceptance of funds	0
No definite policy	0

Funding policy re: Municipal Government:

Acceptance of funds	100
Non-acceptance of funds	0
No policy	0

Funding policy re: Corporate/Private Sources:

Acceptance of funds	100
Non-acceptance of funds	0
No policy	0

Funding policy re: Non-profit sources:

Acceptance of funds	100
Non-acceptance of funds	0
No policy	0

Percent of organizations receiving funds from various sources:

Source	Amount of Funds Received (Percent)							
	0	1-10	11-25	26-50	51-75	76-99	100	Avg.
Government	10	0	10	30	10	40	0	54.2
Organization activity	60	10	10	20	0	0	0	10.0
Private sector	60	10	10	20	0	0	0	12.0
Non-profit orgs	70	30	0	0	0	0	0	1.7

Security of Core funding:

Secure	20
Fairly secure	70
Not assured	10

Security of Program/Project funding:

Secure	0
Fairly secure	22
Not assured	78

Total 1983 expenditure budget:

Under $50,000	11
$50 to $100,000	0
$101 to $300,000	11
$301 to $1 million	44
$1 to $3 million	33
$3 to $10 millin	0
over $10 million	0

Research Institutes

Organizational type—Research Institutes

Year established:

Average	1973
Median	1975
Range	1961 to 1983

Importance of specified activities to organization's purpose (in percent):

Activity	Most Imp.	2	3	4	5	6	N/A	Ave.
Service to benefit population	0	0	0	0	0	0	100	0.0
Service to members	29	14	14	0	0	0	43	1.8
Promotion of Prog/policy change	0	14	43	14	0	0	29	3.0
Education of public	13	25	0	38	13	0	13	3.1
Education of professionals	0	55	36	0	0	0	9	2.4
Policy research	64	14	14	7	0	0	0	1.6

Average percent of Organization time spent on selected activities:

Organization Maintenance	8
Service Delivery	6
Group Liaison	3
Informal Government Liaison	4
Formal Government Liaison	2
Social Research	45
Information Dissemination	18
Miscellaneous	14

Perceived effectiveness of activities on influencing Government social policy (percent).

Activity	Very Effec	2	Effec	4	Not Effec	DK	Not Done	Ave.
Service Delivery	13	25	0	0	0	0	63	1.7
Group Liaison	13	0	0	25	25	0	38	3.8
Informal Govt Liaison	0	11	44	11	0	11	22	3.0
Formal Govt Liaison	0	25	13	25	0	13	25	3.0
Social Policy Research	7	36	36	7	0	7	7	2.5
Information Dissemination	0	23	62	8	0	0	8	2.8

Percentage of Research Institutes attempting to influence social policy = 73.3

How Research Institutes try to influence social policy:

Activity	Percent Mention
Research on social issues	64
Information dissemination	55
Publications and editorials	36
Issue reports	36
Briefs and position papers	27
Conferences	27

Staffing (percentage in each row equals 100):

| Type of Staff | Number of Employees | | | | | |
	0	1-9	10-29	30-49	50-99	100+
Full time professional	15	62	23	0	0	0
Full time support	8	77	8	0	0	0
Contract workers	100	0	0	0	0	0
Casual employees	100	0	0	0	0	0
Volunteers	49	12	---25---		0	12
Total staff	0	54	---23---		0	8

Funding policy re: Federal Government:

Acceptance of funds	69
Non-acceptance of funds	0
No definite policy	31

Funding policy re: Provincial Government:

Acceptance of funds	69
Non-acceptance of funds	0
No definite policy	31

Funding policy re: Municipal Government:

Acceptance of funds	69
Non-acceptance of funds	0
No policy	31

Funding policy re: Corporate/Private Sources:

Acceptance of funds	75
Non-acceptance of funds	0
No policy	25

Funding policy re: Non-profit sources:

Acceptance of funds	75
Non-acceptance of funds	0
No policy	25

Percent of organizations receiving funds from various sources:

Source	Amount of Funds Received (Percent)							
	0	1-10	11-25	26-50	51-75	76-99	100	Avg.
Government	31	19	0	63	13	19	6	36.7
Organization activity	38	38	19	6	0	0	0	7.4
Private sector	56	31	6	0	0	6	0	7.9
Non-profit orgs	69	25	6	0	0	0	0	3.2

Security of Core funding:

Secure	15
Fairly secure	54
Not assured	31

Security of Program/Project funding:

Secure	0
Fairly secure	21
Not assured	9

Total 1983 expenditure budget:

Under $50,000	20
$50 to $100,000	7
$101 to $300,000	40
$301 to $1 million	27
$1 to $3 million	7
$3 to $10 millin	0
over $10 million	0

Service Organizations

Organizational type—Service Organizations

Year established:

Average	1957
Median	1960
Range	1851 to 1978

Importance of specified activities to organization's purpose (in percent):

Activity	Most Imp.	2	3	4	5	6	N/A	Ave.
Service to benefit population	78	6	0	6	0	0	9	1.3
Service to members	11	18	4	4	14	4	46	3.1
Promotion of Prog/policy change	10	45	23	16	0	3	3	2.6
Education of public	9	22	53	13	0	3	0	2.8
Education of professionals	0	4	8	20	28	4	36	4.3
Policy research	7	3	7	24	14	10	34	4.0

Average percent of Organization time spent on selected activities:

Organization Maintenance	14
Service Delivery	41
Group Liaison	4
Informal Government Liaison	3
Formal Government Liaison	7
Social Research	3
Information Dissemination	10
Miscellaneous	18

Perceived effectiveness of activities on influencing Government social policy (percent).

Activity	Very Effec	2	Effec	4	Not Effec	DK	Not Done	Ave.
Service Delivery	15	12	26	18	6	12	12	2.8
Group Liaison	0	14	31	25	0	6	14	3.4
Informal Govt Liaison	19	19	41	6	0	3	13	2.4
Formal Govt Liaison	15	33	21	9	6	9	6	2.5
Social Policy Research	6	22	22	16	3	13	19	2.8
Information Dissemination	6	9	25	25	13	13	9	3.4

Percentage of Service Organizations attempting to influence social policy = 82.9

How Service Organizations try to influence social policy:

Activity	Percent Mention
Briefs and position papers	48
Formal liaison	45
Service delivery activities	38
Group liaison	35
Informal liaison with government	28
Research on social issues	21

Staffing (percentage in each row equals 100):

Type of Staff	Number of Employees					
	0	1-9	10-29	30-49	50-99	100+
Full time professional	15	29	15	25	21	6
Full time support	23	29	23	14	6	9
Contract workers	97	0	0	0	0	3
Casual employees	97	0	0	0	0	3
Volunteers	13	7	---23---		10	47
Total staff	0	12	---23---		18	48

Funding policy re: Federal Government:

Acceptance of funds	81
Non-acceptance of funds	3
No definite policy	16

Funding policy re: Provincial Government:

Acceptance of funds	76
Non-acceptance of funds	7
No definite policy	17.

Funding policy re: Municipal Government:

Acceptance of funds	69
Non-acceptance of funds	7
No policy	24

Funding policy re: Corporate/Private Sources:

Acceptance of funds	80
Non-acceptance of funds	0
No policy	20

Funding policy re: Non-profit sources:

Acceptance of funds	77
Non-acceptance of funds	3
No policy	20

Percent of organizations receiving funds from various sources:

Source	Amount of Funds Received (Percent)							
	0	1-10	11-25	26-50	51-75	76-99	100	Avg.
Government	14	0	19	11	11	31	14	55
Organization activity	28	39	8	17	6	3	0	16
Private sector	47	31	8	6	0	6	3	12
Non-profit orgs	50	25	8	8	3	0	0	9

Security of Core funding:

Secure	38
Fairly secure	42
Not assured	20

Security of Program/Project funding:

Secure	6
Fairly secure	39
Not assured	55

Total 1983 expenditure budget:

Under $50,000	12
$50 to $100,000	6
$101 to $300,000	12
$301 to $1 million	15
$1 to $3 million	15
$3 to $10 millin	24
over $10 million	15

METHODOLOGY

One of the main objectives of the study was to identify the various types of actors, the roles they play and the methods they employ. In order to achieve this objective, a broad range of data had to be collected, in some cases at the expense of greater depth of information. The information collected can be classified under a number of sub-headings which reflect the above purpose:

1. General confirmation or rejection of the hypothesis that there exists a recognizable social policy process.
2. General confirmation or rejection of the hypothesis that there exists an identifiable social policy network and, should it exist, the identification of its members.
3. Construction of an inventory of organizations against which a typology could be tested to determine its ability to differentiate among organizations.
4. Identification of the various type of activities engaged in by organizations, and the perceived impact of these activities on government social policy.
5. Assessment of the interaction between funding sources and organizational activities and between funding sources and the perceived impact of organizational activities on social policy.

The Literature Search

A short but intensive search of the literature was undertaken during the first six weeks of the study. This literature search revealed not only a suggested typology for classifying organizations but also a number of factors which would limit the reliability of the study. A problem encountered by all studies in this field has been the identification of the appropriate target population. The number of organizations which can, with justification, state that they have an interest in the development of social policy has been estimated at between 10,000 and 15,000. To our knowledge, no one has actually catalogued the field and the total population of NGOs from which to draw the sample is unknown and perhaps unknowable.

The major problem in identifying relevant NGOs arises from the dynamic and transient nature of many of the organizations. It is a common observation that organizations crystallize around particular and current issues but this initial focus frequently shifts over time as public interest in the initiating issue wanes and the subsequent shift of focus may take several forms. The issues of importance to the organization may change or there may be an expansion from one or two specific topics to several more general ones.

An associated problem encountered in trying to select a suitable sample is an inability to judge the type of organization and its interests from the organization's name. Initial interests or foci are frequently implied by the original name but while the foci change over time, the name of the organization is usually changed with some reluctance.

Another problem in sample selection is organizational transience. Many organizations appear to fade away after one or two years -- often as a result of the loss of public interest or the loss of the organization's initiator and catalyst. A number of questionnaires were returned with entries to the effect "Organization folded".

Frequent changes in the leadership of the organizations are also a matter of concern. For the present survey, it was decided to try to contact the ranking operational person in each organization, usually the Executive Director. However, several questionnaires were returned as a result of the named person no longer being with the organization.

Nearly half of the questionnaires returned had errors in the address because small NGOs tend to move fairly frequently.

The central problem, about which there is general consensus in the literature, relates to the depth and breadth of organizations which could, with justification, say that they had an interest in social policy. Any criteria devised would in some ways be arbitrary and difficult to apply in particular cases. Organizations in the social policy field tend to have multiple interests and means.

Identification of the Target Group for Interviews and Questionnaires

In order to provide both the breadth and depth required, a two-pronged approach was adopted. Breadth was to be provided by a questionnaire; depth by structured interviews. To obtain a broadly representative and meaningful initial foothold in the field, a group of seventeen individuals considered to be experienced and knowledgeable in the social policy field were asked to name those organizations which they felt were most influential in terms of social policy. Forty-eight organizations were identified and these became the core group around which the interview selection occurred and from which the initial list of questionnaire respondents was built.

Analysis of the initial list of 48 organizations identified a pattern of organizational types as well as influential organizations. As some of the initially identified organizations could not be interviewed for a variety of reasons, this pattern was translated into the criteria for interview selection. These criteria resulted in the following sample selection:

- Inclusion of all of the large, umbrella organizations with research and advocacy responsibilities in a broad range of areas. These included international, national and regional organizations with many interests in the entire welfare services field.
- Under the following sub-fields of social policy, one national organization and two provincial organizations were approached (with some attempt at regional balance). In some cases, because of long standing professional or ideological dilemmas associated with the sub-field, a selection which accommodated those differences was considered more important than a regional balance. At the provincial and local level, several consumer and service delivery groups were included to achieve balance within the social policy field. The list of interviewed organizations by their field is presented in Table A1.
- Local planning councils: These organizations are very active at the local level but do not have a formally recognized position in the hierarchical structure that applies consistently throughout the country.
  Their involvement in community development and advocacy is significant but varies a great deal in terms of resources and activities. A sample of seven, regionally distributed, were chosen for the interview sample from a list provided by the Canadian Council on Social Development.

Table 1: Fields of Social Policy to be Interviewed

Subfield	Number	Level
Health (traditional)	1	National
	1	Quebec
	1	Western province
Health (alternative)	1	provincial
Housing	1	Co-op housing
	1	Home builder's lobby
Natives	1	Native Indian (national)
	1	Inuit (national)
	1	Metis (provincial)

Women	1	national lobby
	1	national research group
	2	local committees
Children and Youth	1	national
	2	provincial
Elderly	1	national
	2	provincial
Disabled	1	national
	2	provincial
The Poor	2	provincial

- Labour, business and religious organizations were also interviewed regarding their social policy activities. Size and representatives were the criteria used to identify these respondents.
- Professional associations were selected using the criterion of national organizations with a regional balance of provincial arms. This criterion resulted in the selection of organizations associated with doctors, nurses and social workers.
- Professional schools were restricted to schools of social work with a known interest in the development of social policy (as opposed to schools with a focus on developing individual professional techniques). Two of these schools were chosen from those identified as influential by the first set of respondents. The criterion of regional balance was applied, one each in a western and eastern province.
- Research institutes were sampled on the basis of the reactions of the first set of respondents. Four organizations were selected.
- Government officials were sampled from: the departments of Health and Welfare Canada and Indian and Northern Affairs Canada; Provincial departments of social services at the deputy minister level (again regionally distributed); and from the directors of Municipal social planning departments, regionally distributed. A total of 7 federal officials were interviewed, 5 provincial officials, and 4 municipal.

In the process of coordinating travel plans, seven members of the selected sample were unable to be interviewed. In addition, several other influential individuals were identified by early interviewees and this led to some substitutions and adjustments. In the end, interviews of 1 to 1.5 hours each were conducted by two interviewers using common, pre-structured pre-tested interview plans.

The list of questionnaire addressees was developed from a variety of sources, including the responses of the 17 'knowledgeable individuals'. Other sources of names included task force and commission reports (1980-84), both federal and provincial; records of appearances before federal standing committees of the House and Senate; a list of participants from the Secretariat to the Macdonald Commission; directories available from organizations such as CCSD and SPARC of BC; Veterans Affairs Canada (Sources); guides to granting agencies, guides to associations and lists of contributors. The selection criteria included the following:

- A demonstrated interest in social policy: i.e., have made a presentation to a government body or task force over the past 4 years or have been identified as interested and influential in social policy by another organization.

- A balance of organizations from the following areas:
  - municipal, provincial and national spheres of interest
  - subject areas of interest: old age, children, families, health, pensions, women's issues, community development, labour, business and professional development.
  - types of organizations: Advisory or Planning Councils, Business Organizations, Interest Groups or Coalitions of Interest Groups, Labour Organizations, Professional Associations, Religious Organizations, Research Institutes, Service Delivery or Self-help Groups, Professional Schools and Funding Agencies.
  - geographical location of organization.

It should be noted that certain types of groups and individuals have not been surveyed though they are clearly part of the social policy community. These include: politicians; editors of policy magazines; media representatives who specialize in social policy; political party representatives; leaders of single-interest groups.

The final sample size was 535. This total was arrived at through a series of iterations each of which added to and then culled from the target group on the basis of the criteria mentioned above.

Design of the Instruments

A great deal of effort and time was spent in the design of the questionnaire, particularly in the generation of questions which would be meaningful to a broad spectrum of respondents. Compromises had to be made which resulted in some questions being either not applicable or difficult for some types of organization to answer. To offset this problem, an open-answer response option was included in most questions, permitting unanticipated responses to be made within an established structure.

Terminology was also problematic, in part because of the inevitable ambiguity associated with technical terms used in colloquial Canadian English. The meaning of words such as "policy", "programs" and "project"; words describing activities such as "liaison with government", "research" and "information dissemination"; and words used to describe inter-organizational relationships such as "federation", "coalition", "sister group", "parent institution", etc., are neither clearly defined nor consistent in their meaning amongst the organizations. This made it difficult to design questions in a way which would make them equivalent for a wide variety of respondents, but where inter-organizational agreement on terms was considered crucial, definitions were provided.

The questionnaire went through several revisions with pretesting between each although the final version, could not be pretested in its entirety due to time pressures.

The questionnaire was sent in both French and English, but translation also proved to be problematic due to the imprecise nature of the terminology. The translators into French had to consult several times with those who drafted the English version in order to ascertain the sense of the words used and there was debate between the translators as to the correct terms. Small changes in the layout occurred as a result of the translation but the order and basic structure of the questions remained intact.

Interviews were structured. Two types of response sheets, one for NGOs and a second for government officials, were devised and provided to the interviewers. The format of the interviews centered around the identification of a concrete example taken from the respondent's personal experience. Relevant information was then drawn from this example and an attempt was then made to generalize this information by asking the interviewee whether or not the pattern or process identified in the specific example was the usual pattern of events.

Inter-interviewer standardization was sought by initially performing joint interviews, followed by discussion and agreement over how responses might best be classified.

Delivery of the Test Instrument

Those who were to be interviewed were contacted ahead of time and asked whether they would like to participate. Those agreeing to be interviewed were provided beforehand with a package of materials outlining the nature of the study and the type of questions which would be asked. A guarantee that the material would remain confidential was considered essential in order to ensure the necessary degree of openness and candour, and this was stressed by the interviewers especially in the case of civil servants.

The questionnaire was sent to the respondents with a package of material including a covering letter asking for their assistance, a Background Note explaining the nature of the study,* and a stamped return envelope. The covering letter also included the name and phone number of a contact person in IRPP for those seeking additional information.

The questionnaire package was mailed out on August 11. A follow-up letter was sent on September 4 to those who had not responded by August 31 together with a single sheet brochure on the Institute. The brochure was sent to provide respondents with information about the nature of IRPP, its organization, its funding sources and its independence.

---

* A copy of the Background Note is attached to this report as Appendix A.

QUESTIONNAIRE ANALYSIS

Response Rate

A total of 535 questionnaires were sent out. Twenty-nine were returned address unknown. There were 183 responses, 10 of which were intentionally not filled in by the respondent. Thus, the overall rate of return was 34.2 percent.

A number of respondents cited the length of the questionnaire and the time required to gather the information needed to complete it as reasons for a delayed return. More respondents, however, mentioned the time of year ("I happened to be on vacation when it arrived and just got back") as the reason for the delay. This reasoning is supported by the number of returns (20.8 percent of total sample) mailed in the week after the Labour Day Weekend (shortly before the follow-up letter arrived). Undoubtedly, the calling of a federal election also resulted in fewer returns as organizations may have used the opportunity provided by the election to talk with or lobby various would-be MPs. It should also be noted that 55.2 percent of the returned and filled-in questionnaires indicated that there were errors in the mailing labels, more than half in the name of the respondent.

The reasons given by those returning but not filling in the questionnaire were:

- the questionnaire does not seem to apply (N=3)
- another organization closely aligned to us also received a questionnaire and there would be very little difference between their response and our own (N=2)
- we are now amalgamated (N=2)

- we are afraid of government reprisal (N=1)
- we don't want to be included (N=2).

Quality of Questionnaire Response

Coders were asked to evaluate the reliability and completeness of each questionnaire. While 13.1 percent of the questionnaires were judged to be "somewhat unreliable", none was judged to be so unreliable as to exclude it. Four percent of the questionnaires were incomplete, these were included as the procedures automatically excluded 'non-responses' for individual questions from the statistical calculations.

Representativeness of the Responses

Eleven different types of organizations were identified by the questionnaire. Given the total number of returns, this resulted in only three categories being sufficiently well represented (N less than 30) to make generalizations to their sub-field population. However, even for these classifications great caution would have to be exercised in generalizing, given the fact that the total population was and remains unknown and thus random sampling was not possible.

The extent to which those classifications having less than thirty respondents can be considered to be representative is clearly limited. Consequently, only descriptive statistics are used in the comparisons made in the analysis.

The number of respondents per classification is given in Table 1. Note that the size of three categories: religious, the non-profit funding organizations, and federal granting agencies were considered too small to support any valid observations and are therefore omitted from further analysis.

Table 1: Respondents by organizational category

Type of Organization	Respondents
Advisory or Planning Council	30
Business Organization	8
Interest Group or Coalition	45
Labour Organization	10
Non-profit Funding Organizations	4
Professional Association	19
Professional School	10
Religious Organization	3
Research Institute	16
Service Delivery and Self-Help Group	36
Federal Granting Agency	2
Total	183

A possible sampling bias is evident only in the advisory organizations category. In this category, 17 of the 30 respondents are Social Planning Councils from Ontario. Consequently there may be some bias here, departing from a national perspective towards an emphasis on circumstances in Ontario.

There is positive skewing in the services and labour sub-groups due to the respective inclusion of one and two very large organizations with a majority of smaller ones. Other than in these classifications, skewing does not seem to be a major problem.

In terms of national distribution, each telephone area code except that of Northern Ontario and Eastern Quebec had a respondent. The majority of respondents were in area code 416 (Southern Ontario—27.3 percent, followed by 613 (Ottawa—16.4 percent). The least represented province was Newfoundland with two respondents.

Each political level of organization (International, National, Provincial and Municipal) is represented. The breakdown of these levels is presented in Table 2.

Table 2: Level of Government of Interest to Organizations

Level of Operation	Number of Organizations
International	3
National	40
Provincial	84
Municipal	13
Both International and National	2
Both National and Provincial	18
International, National and Provincial	2
National, Provincial and Municipal	12
Territorial	1
Regional	2

Organizational Establishment

By taking the age of the various types of organizations by category, a table (Table 3) giving both the average and median years by organizational type can be created. This table may give an indication of the evolutionary pattern of the various types of NGOs in Canada. (Caution has to be exercised given the sample size.) If we examine the first column, average year organization established, we note the following temporal progression of organization types: Labour (1945), Professional Associations (1947), Service (1956), Business (1960), Professional Schools (1963), Advisory Councils (1963), Interest Groups (1965), and Research Institutes (1973).

The newest type or organization is the research institute (established mean 1973) whereas the oldest responding research institute was established in 1961.

Table 3: Average and Median Years of Organization Establishment
(by organizational type)

Type of organization	Average year organizational type established	Median year organizational type established
Labour	1945	1955
Professional Association	1947	1950
Service	1957	1960
Business	1960*	1958*
Professional School	1963*	1971
Advisory	1963	1971
Interest	1965*	1972
Research	1973	1975

* outlier removed

Only 5 respondents (31.3 percent) were established prior to 1970. Fifty percent were established after 1974. Research institutes are "the new kid on the block".

Most organization types appear to demonstrate a relatively stable pattern of development and organizational longevity as shown by a small degree of negative skew—part of which can be attributed to an increase in population. The extreme case of skew is the service group. There the larger number of recent versus older organizations may indicate that either there is a greater chance of organizational failure in these types or that there has been a relatively recent and rapid expansion in these fields.

Benefit Groups and Membership

A number of questions were asked about the size of membership and the benefit population but the answers to these questions are hard to compare because of the heterogeneity of respondents. While some organizations could identify a quantifiable benefit group, such as individuals and families, others could only identify other groups, institutions, agencies, communities, and the general public. Consequently, any comparison that might be attempted would lead to erroneous conclusions.

Organizational Purpose

A ranking of activities regarded as important to the organization's purpose was requested, using an open-ended scale with "1" being most important. It had six purposes explicitly identified, and room for two "other" purposes. For the discussion below, 4 categories were arbitrarily established using this scale.

These are: 1.0 to 1.5, very important; 1.6 to 2.5, important; 2.6 to 3.5, somewhat important; and 3.6+, not important.

Service to a benefit population, the first provided purpose, was seen as very important only to service organizations (Mean = 1.3). The other types of organizations saw service as either somewhat important with Professional Associations ranking service to a benefit population at 3.5, Advisory Groups at 3.7 and Interest at 3.0, or as "not important" with Professional Schools and Business ranking service at a mean of 4.0 and Labour at a mean of 4.6. Research Institutes considered service to benefit group as "not applicable".

Service to Members was ranked as very important by Labour (Mean = 1.3). Professional Schools (Mean = 2.0), Professional Associations (Mean = 2.1), Business Organizations (Mean = 1.6), and Research Institutes (Mean = 1.8) saw this activity as "important". The remainder saw this activity as somewhat important: Interest Groups (Mean = 2.8), Service Organizations (Mean = 3.1), and Advisory Councils (Mean = 3.4).

The education of the public was viewed as "important" only by Interest Groups (Mean = 2.3). The remaining organizations saw education of the public as "somewhat important": Business (Mean = 2.8); Research Institutes (Mean = 3.1); Service (Mean = 2.8); Advisory (Mean = 2.9); and Professional Schools (Mean = 3.4); and, as "not important", by Labour (Mean = 3.9); and Professional Associations (Mean = 3.8).

The education of professionals was viewed as "very important" by Professional Schools (Mean = 1.4) "important" by Research Institutes (Mean = 2.4), "somewhat important" by Business (Mean = 2.7) Professional Associations (Mean = 2.7), and Interest Groups (Mean = 3.3); and as "not important" by Advisory Organizations (Mean = 4.0), Labour (Mean = 3.8) and Service Groups (Mean = 4.3).

Research Institutes, Professional Schools, and Advisory Councils saw policy research as "important" (respective means of 1.6, 2.0, and 2.4). Business saw research as being "somewhat important" (Mean = 2.8) as did Interest Groups (Mean = 3.4). Professional Associations (Mean = 3.9), Service Organizations (Mean = 4.0), and Labour (Mean = 4.2) all ranked research as "not important" to their purpose.

Promotion of policy and program change was considered as "very important" by Business (Mean = 1.4), as "important" by Advisory Groups (Mean = 1.8), Interest Groups (Mean = 2.1), Labour (Mean = 2.4) and Professional Associations (Mean = 2.5) and as somewhat important by the remainder: Service (Mean = 2.6), Professional Schools (Mean = 2.7) and Research Institutes (Mean = 3.0).

Overall, the purpose ranked highest in importance was Policy promotion and change (Mean = 2.3), followed by Service to Members (Mean = 2.5). Service to benefit group, the education of the public, the education of professionals, and policy research all ranked as "somewhat important" with means of 2.6, 2.9, 3.2, and 3.1 respectively.

There are several observations that can be made:

1. Advisory councils and service organizations rank "providing services to members" as the least important to their purpose (Means = 3.4 and 3.1 respectively) and are closely followed in this by Interest Groups (Mean = 2.8). There is then a gap in terms of the perceived importance of this activity up to Professional Associations (Mean = 2.1) Professional Schools (Mean = 2.0), Research (Mean = 1.8), Business (Mean = 1.7), and Labour (Mean = 1.3). The gap gives the impression of a bimodal distribution: the organizations above the gap (Means less than 2.2) appear to be much more concerned with the service they are providing to their members than those below it (Mean greater than 2.7). The three types or organizations below the gap can be thought of as those most outward-oriented: their support comes fom their ability to affect things (policy, programs, etc.) in the larger environment that their members cannot alter for themselves. The support does not stem from the services they provide either to their membership or their benefit group, as is the case of those organizations on the other side of the gap.

2. The number of organizations responding to each category of activity varies. For example, 11 Advisory Organizations answered the question about the importance of service to a benefit group, while 17 answered the question about the importance of service to members, and 25 answered the question about promotion of policy or program change. This variation in the number of respondents is consistent across all types of organizations. One implication is that some purposes were viewed as "Not Applicable" by some respondents. Given that the intent of the question was to rank activities in terms of their importance, a choice of "Not Applicable" might be considered as the least possible level of importance. One would expect to find, then, that activities receiving a low mean ranking, i.e., greater than 3.5, would also be those receiving the most N/A's and for the most part, this pattern holds. Where it does not hold, i.e.: few N/A's and low ranking, the responding organizations would be indicating an activity which most engaged in, yet regarded as unimportant. There are, in total, 4 instances where this happened and they occurred in two categories of purposes. Both Labour and Professional Associations rank the education of the public as 'unimportant' (means of 3.9 and 3.8 respectively), yet this activity was ranked by 90% of the labour organizations and 94.7% of the professional associations. Similarly, policy research is indicated as an activity by 77.8% of interest groups yet ranked as 'unimportant' at 3.4. The final occurrence of this pattern is that of labour organizations, 90% of whom indicated that they undertook policy research but ranked it at 4.5. It would seem that these activities are viewed as necessary expenditures though distantly related to the organization's purpose.

Types Attempting Social Policy Influence

A question was asked as to whether or not the respondent attempted to influence social policy. Ninety percent of the organizations stated that they did attempt to influence social policy: eight percent said they did not and 1.6 percent said they 'did not know'. A breakdown by organization type of those stating that they did not attempt to influence policy is shown in Table 4.

Table 4: Percentages of those Organization Types Not Attempting to Influence Policy

Type of Organization	Percent Not Attempting Influence
Advisory	7.1
Business	0.0
Interest	2.2
Labour	0.0
Professional Association	0.0
Research Institute	26.7
Service	14.3
Professional School	10.0

Effectiveness of Activities in Influencing Social Policy

In order to gauge the perceived effectiveness in influencing government social policy of various activities commonly performed by most NGOs, a five point scale was created, reading: 1 = very effective; 3 = effective, 5 = not effective at all. Exclusion options of 9 = Don't Know and 0 = Not done by this organization, were also provided. The activities to be rated were:

A. Service Delivery Activities
B. Liaison with Similar Groups
C. Informal Liaison with Government
D. Formal Liaison with Government
E. Research on Social Issues
F. Information Dissemination

A further category: "G. Other", was also included in order to capture unanticipated activities.

Overall, the activities were rated at 2.8, slightly higher than "effective". The range of mean responses by type or organization and type of activity ran from a high of 1.8 to a low of 3.8. Within each type of organization, there appeared to be little general consensus on the effectiveness of the various activities. The entire range of responses was commonly indicated.

This suggests that either the organizations do not know what is effective or that the effectiveness of certain activities is dependent on the composition of particular organizations. As with organizational purposes, the number of respondents varied from cell to cell in terms of the perceived effectiveness for the particular type of organization. For example, 17 Advisory Organizations responded to the effectiveness of service delivery activities, whereas 25 responded to the question on the effectiveness of information dissemination.

Informal Liaison with Government was rated highest overall, i.e., most effective (Mean = 2.55) closely followed by Research on Social Issues (Mean = 2.72). Formal Government Liaison rated third (Mean = 2.75), Information Dissemination came fourth (Mean = 2.84), then Service Delivery (Mean = 2.93) and finally Group Liaison (Mean = 2.95).

Service delivery was rated lowest by 4 of the 8 types of organizations, including: Advisory (Mean = 3.18), Interest Groups (Mean = 2.88), Labour (Mean = 3.57) and Professional Associations (Mean = 3.36). The remainder rated service delivery in the middle range of their individual rankings. The highest rating was given by Business (Mean = 1.83).

Group liaison activities were not rated lowest in effectiveness by any type of organization. However, no type of organization rated this activity highly. Of the 6 options given, four organizational types rated Group Liaison fifth in effectiveness and three rated it fourth. This fact suggests that, at the NGO level, working with other organizations is not seen as an important means of influencing social policy. These results lend support to the view that at the NGO level there may be a service network but not a policy network.

Information dissemination was the activity which split the organizational types most dramatically. Two rated it lowest in effectiveness, 1 at second lowest, 1 at second most effective and 2 at most effective. Those giving information dissemination a high effectiveness rating include Interest Groups (Mean = 2.34—the highest rating given by this type); Labour (Mean = 2.75—the highst rating given by this type); and Professional Associations (Mean = 2.69—second highest rating given by this type, the highest was 2.35). Those rating Information Dissemination as least effective were Service Groups (Mean = 3.36—lowest rating by this type), Business Organizations (Mean = 3.40—lowest rating by this type) and Advisory Councils (Mean = 3.04—second lowest by this type—lowest was 3.18).

The reason for this split is not apparent from the questionnaire or interview responses. However, its occurrence might suggest that certain types of groups are less able to make their views known to government, and resort to altering public opinion as the best means of having undesirable policy changed. Advisory councils and service groups can be expected to have closer ties to government, given the nature of their work and the fact that amongst the types of organizations surveyed (excluding Professional Schools, most of which are attached to universities) they receive the highest percentage of funds from government (45.4 percent for Advisory Councils and 55.3 percent for service organizations). In contrast to Advisory and Service Organizations, those rating information dissemination as most effective receive on average 25.4 percent of their funding from government (34.0 percent for interest groups, 3.5 percent for Labour and 17.2 percent for Professional Associations).

The other type of organization rating information dissemination as the least effective means of influencing policy were business organizations (Mean = 3.4). They receive an average of 15.3 percent of direct funding from government. There is nothing in the questionnaire to suggest why business rated information dissemination so low. However, it should be noted that this type of organization also rated formal and informal liaison with government highest in terms of what was viewed as the best means of affecting social policy. This may indicate that Business finds these channels so effective as to minimize the need to appeal to the general public.

It should also be noted that the other two types of organization which viewed information dissemination as relatively ineffective (Advisory and Service) also saw liaison with government as more effective.

Only Advisory Councils ranked policy research as most effective (Mean = 2.61) though 3 other types ranked it second: Research Institutes (Mean = 2.50), Interest Groups (Mean = 2.54) and Labour (Mean = 2.88). Excluding Labour, these responses could be generally anticipated given the nature of the organizations. What was not anticipated is that no organization rated research lowest. This result will be discussed below.

The final two categories of activities are formal and informal liaison with government. Overall, these categories were rated third and first in effectiveness, respectively, with all types of organization ranking informal liaison as more effective in changing policy than formal liaison (grouped mean of 2.55 for informal liaison versus 2.75 for formal liaison).

In terms of average rating by type, Labour Organizations, Professional Schools, and Service Groups rated that activities offered lowest in effectiveness in influencing social policy, giving them an average rating of 3.11, 2.88, and 2.84 respectively. These ratings are closely followed by most of the other organizational types: Professional Associations (Mean = 2.84), Research Institutes (Mean = 2.70), Advisory (Mean = 2.82), and Interest Groups (Mean = 2.64). The group that felt most sure of its ability to influence government social policy was Business (Mean = 2.49).

The range of mean responses for the influential activities varied between 0.54 for Interest Groups and 1.57 for Business Organizations. The average range of responses for each type was 0.98.

Influential Activities Undertaken

Having determined which activities organizations found to be effective, an open question was asked regarding which activities were undertaken by the respondent given that they were attempting to influence social policy. A total of six activities were indicated by over 20 percent of those answering the question. The activity most engaged in by those trying to influence policy was the presentation of briefs and position papers (49 percent of those answering the question). Thirty-two percent of those respondents which indicated that they presented briefs and position papers came from interest groups, 21 percent from service organizations, 15.7 percent from advisory councils, 13 percent from professional associations, 6.9 percent from business, 4 percent from both labour and research institutes, and 2 percent from professional schools.

The other 5 major activities in order of reported frequency were: formal liaison with Government (36.2 percent), group liaison (32.9 percent), information dissemination (30.9 percent), research on social issues (28.2 percent), and informal liaison with government (26.2 percent). It is interesting to note that while organizations purport to recognize the effectiveness of informal liaison with Government, only about one-quarter of the organizations reported that they engaged in this activity. This suggests that organizations face barriers which prevent them from doing what they believe to be most effective in influencing social policy.

Similarly, a discrepancy exists between the perceived effectiveness of group liaison and the degree to which it is engaged in. Though rated as the least effective of the optional activities in terms of influencing social policy, it was the third most frequently mentioned activity of organizations.

Different types of organizations stressed different methods of influencing social policy. Advisory Councils mentioned briefs and position papers (39 percent) and informal liaison with government, along with research on social issues (both at 35 percent). Business ranked the presentation of briefs and position papers and formal liaison with government first (57 percent) followed by research on social issues, meeting with government authorities or officials, and public meetings (each with 29 percent). Interest groups indicated that the major means of influencing policy was through the presentation of briefs and position papers (56 percent) followed by liaison with similar groups and formal liaison with government (39 percent), public awareness through the media (28 percent), informal liaison with government (26 percent), and information dissemination (26 percent).

Labour indicated information dissemination as the means most often used to influence social policy (70 percent) followed by group liaison (50 percent), formal liaison with government (40 percent) and then group coalitions, briefs and position papers, research on social issues, and public awareness through the media (all mentioned by 30 percent of. this organizational type). Professional associations scored formal liaison with government highest at 63 percent, followed by briefs and position papers (56 percent), information dissemination (38 percent), informal liaison with government (31 percent), group liaison (31 percent), and research on social issues (19 percent).

Research Institutes stressed research on social issues as their major activity with respect to influencing social policy (64 percent), and mentioned information dissemination (55 percent), publications and editorials (36 percent), reports (36 percent), briefs and position papers (27 percent), and conferences (27 percent). Service organizations mentioned the presentation of briefs and position papers most frequently (48 percent), followed by formal liaison with government (45 percent), service delivery (30 percent), group liaison

(35 percent), informal liaison with government (28 percent) and research on social issues (21 percent). Professional schools reported engaging in research on social issues (50 percent), service delivery activities (25 percent), informal liaison with government (25 percent), formal liaison with government (25 percent), and information dissemination (25 percent).

Budgets

Organizations were asked to report their 1983 expenditure budgets. These figures were then groupd into seven classifications. The overall results are shown in Table 5.

Table 5: Overall Range of Budgets Reported

Budget Range (in thousands)	Number Reporting	Percent
Under $50	34	18.6
$50 to $100	14	7.7
$101 to $300	35	19.1
$301 to $1000	37	20.2
$1001 to $3000	15	8.2
$3001 to $10000	19	10.4
over $10000	11	6.0
No response	18	9.8

A breakdown of average budgets by organization type is shown in Table 6. The two largest average budgets are those of labour and service. While the size of these budgets was unexpectedly large, neither distribution shows an unusually large amount of skew. There are no noticeable outliers.

Table 6: Average 1983 Budget by Organizational Type

Type of Organization	Average Reported Budget (in thousands)
Advisory	1,209.3
Business	1,237.9
Interest	727.7
Labour	9,662.9
Professional Association	630.7
Professional School	781.4
Research	402.3
Service	4,338.6*

*Outlier removed

It was anticipated that there would be a positive skewing of the budgets with many poorly funded organizations and a few well funded ones, but this pattern is not as general as was expected, however. It is clearly pronounced only in interest groups, though noticeable in advisory councils. In both cases the skewing, being positive, would suggest that there is some organizational instability. While there is no further evidence in the questionnaire of instability amongst advisory councils, several interest groups clearly lack sufficient funding to continue. This view is supported by several unsolicited comments written in by members of the type against the budget question. One such comment read: "We are desperately short of funding."

In looking at the budget distribution amongst interest groups (Table 7) it is interesting to note that the distribution would be considerably less skewed after the initial category "under $50000" was surpassed. The $50000 figure, then, might be considered as the change point between those organizations which have attained some stability and those that may fall by the wayside.

Table 7: Distribution of 1983 Expenditure Budget for Interest Group

Budget Category (in thousands)	Frequency	Percent
Under $50	14	31.1
$50 to $100	5	11.1
$101 to $300	8	17.8
$300 to $1000	5	11.1
$1000 to $3000	3	6.7
$3001 to $10000	5	11.1

Funding Security

The above interpretation of the interest group's insecurity with respect to funding is also supported by the responses given to the two questions about the security of funding. The responses had a range of 1 to 3, with the option of indicating "Don't Know". Interest groups and business rated their security of core funding second lowest, with a Mean of 2.01. Only research institutions rated core funding security lower at a Mean of 2.23. The most secure type or organization was Labour (Mean = 1.4), followed by professional associations (Mean = 1.6), service (Mean = 1.8) and professional schools and advisory councils (Mean = 1.9).

Full-time Salaried Professionals

In terms of another organizational resource, full-time salaried professionals, all types of organization showed some degree of positive skew in the distribution. All types or organization except research had noticeable outliers—particular organizations whose professional staff size was over twice the size of the next highest organization. This is shown in Table 8. The size of this gap is interesting in itself. It would seem to indicate that within each type or organization, there are a few which are truly large organizations.* It is important to recognize at this point that most of these organizations engage in social policy only as a sideline to their major purpose: e.g., professional schools educate. Therefore, the large staff size may have no bearing on the influence of these organizations on social policy.

Table 8: Full-time Professional Staff by Organization Type Showing Gap Between Highest Number Reported and the Next Highest

Type of Organization	Highest Number of Full-time Professional Staff	Next to Highest
Advisory	60	23
Business	30	5
Interest	98	30
Labour	235 and 200	70
Professional Associations	100	27
Professional Schools	70	19
Research	18	10
Service	929	453

Excluding the relatively large respondent organizations, a degree of positive skewness in full-time professional staff can be observed only in one organizational type, namely interest groups. As mentioned earlier, under the topic of budgetary size, such positive skewing may indicate instability in this organizational type. There may be more new organizations forming and dissolving on a regular basis. Information mentioned above which supports this view is the relative newness of this organizational type: over half of the members in this category were established after 1971.

Funding Policy

Organizations were asked about their funding policy with respect to accepting funds from various sources. One of the interesting aspects of the responses received was the clear indication that many respondents did not know what was meant by "funding policy". Approximately 30 percent of those responding included non-policy statements, such as:

> Grants and/or donations for specific services and programs are appreciated and accepted.

---

* It would be interesting to study the relative influence of large versus small organizations on social policy. The preliminary nature of the present study precluded questions on the influence on policy of specific organizations.

Major funding source: provincial government.
Minor funding source: university bequests.
Minor funding source: student fees.

No policy

We have applied and got grants for special projects from federal and provincial governments.... Normal services are fully financed through per capita of our affiliates.

We operate a _____ service which generated revenues for our programs.

The most common funding policies included:

Anything offered was accepted.

No funds accepted if used for representational purposes.

No funds accepted where there could be a conflict of interest.

Not all funding from one source.

The major conclusion one can reach from such comments is that many organizations fear losing their independence. They see funding as a means whereby other organizations, including government, can either subvert or divert them from their purpose. As such, this concern reflects the general integrity of these organizations and their desire to fulfil their mandates.

General Comments on Social Policy

When asked to make a general comment on the social policy process, most respondents declined. The comments of those who did respond were diverse, the maximum repetition of a comment being 3 times. The comments which received three "votes" were:

1. Social policy development is reactive rather than proactive.
2. Broader social policy concerns assume secondary importance at both the federal and provincial levels.
3. The federal government neither understands nor practices consultation with NGOs.

General Conclusions

Some of the general conclusions which have been drawn from the foregoing analysis are presented in Appendix B of this Report.

BIBLIOGRAPHY

Akey, Denise S., ed. Encyclopedia of Associations, 1984. Detroit: Gale Research Co., 1983.

Arlett, Allan, ed. Canadian Directory to Foundations and Granting Agencies. Toronto: The Canadian Centre for Philanthropy, 1982.

Armitage, A. Social Sciences and Public Policy in Canada. Toronto: McClelland and Stewart Ltd., 1975.

Armitrage, Andrew Social Welfare in Canada: Ideals and Realities. Toronto: McClelland and Stewart Ltd., 1975.

Atkinson, Michael M. and Marsha A. Chandler, eds. The Politics of Canadian Public Policy. Toronto: University of Toronto Press, 1983.

Baker, Richard J.S. Administrative Theory and Public Administration. London: Hutchinson University Library, 1972.

Blondel, Jean The Organization of Governments: A Comparative Analysis of Government Structures. London: Sage Publications, 1982.

Campbell, Edwin Colin Governments Under Stress: Political Executives and Key Bureaucrats in Washington, London and Ottawa. Toronto: University of Toronto Press, 1983.

Canada. Commission of Inquiry into Part-time Work Part-time Work in Canada: Report of the Commission of Inquiry into Part-time Work. Ottawa: Labour Canada, 1983.

Canada. Department of National Health and Welfare Working Paper on Social Security in Canada. Ottawa: 1973.

Canada. Health and Welfare Canada, 1984-85 Estimates: Part III Expenditure Plan. Ottawa: Minister of Supply and Services, 1984.

Canada. House of Commons Special Committee on the Disabled and the Handicapped. Native Population: Follow-up Report. Ottawa: The Committee, 1981.

Canada. House of Commons Special Committee on the Disabled and the Handicapped. Obstacles: The Third Report (of the) Special Committee on the Disabled and the Handicapped. Ottawa: Minister of Supply and Services, 1981.

Canada. House of Commons Special Committee on Employment Opportunities for the '80s. Work for Tomorrow: Employment Opportunities for the '80s. Ottawa: House of Commons, 1981.

Canada. House of Commons Special Committee on Indian Self-Government in Canada. Minutes of Proceedings of the Special Committee on Indian Self-Government. Ottawa: Queen's printer, 1983.

Canada. Interprovincial Task Force on Social Security (Canada). The Income Security System in Canada: Report prepared by the Interprovincial Task Force on Social Security for the Interprovincial Conference of Ministers Responsible for Social Services. Ottawa, 1980.

Canada. National Council on Welfare. The Working Poor, People and Programs: A Statistical Profile. Ottawa: The Council, 1981.

Canada. Royal Commission on the Economic Union and Development Prospects for Canada. Challenges and Choices. Ottawa: Royal Commission on the Economic Union and Development Prospects for Canada, 1984.

Canada. Special Senate Committee on Poverty. Poverty in Canada: Report of the Special Senate Committee on Poverty. Ottawa: Information Canada, 1971.

Canada. Task Force on Community-Based Residential Centres. Report of the Task Force on Community Based Residential Centres. Ottawa: Solicitor General, Canada, 1973.

Canada. Task Force on the Role of the Private Sector in Criminal Justice. Community Involvement in Criminal Justice, Report of. Ottawa: Minister of Supply and Services, 1977.

Canadian Council on Social Development. Annual Report 1980-1981. Ottawa: 1981.

Canadian Council on Social Development. Directory of Canadian Human Services 1982-83. Ottawa: 1982.

Canadian Council on Social Development. Issues in Canadian Social Policy Reader Volume 7, 1982. Ottawa: 1982.

Canadian Council on Social Development. Proceedings of the Canadian Conference on Social Welfare. Ottawa: 1974.

Canadian Council on Social Development. Social Policies for the Eighties. Ottawa: 1981.

Canadian Council on Social Development. Social Responsibility to Challenge the Future, Canadian Report to the 22nd International Conference on Social Welfare. Montreal: 1984.

Canadian Welfare Council. Social Policies for Canada: A Statement. Ottawa: 1969.

Canadian Welfare Council. Report of the Canadian Committee of the International Council on Social Welfare for the 14th International Conference on Social Welfare, May 1968. Ottawa: Canadian Welfare Council, 1968.

Cooperstock, Henry. Relations Between Local Voluntary Organizations and the Federal Government. Ottawa: Assistance to Community Groups Program, 1977.

DPA Consulting Limited. The Development of a Typology of the Voluntary Sector in Canada. Ottawa: Secretary of State, Policy Coordination Analysis and Management Systems Branch, 1983.

Djao, Angela Wei Inequality and Social Policy: The Sociology of Welfare. Toronto: John Wiley and Sons Ltd. 1983.

Dobell, A. Rodney Social Policy Making in the 1980s: Elements and Issues. Paris: OECD, 1980.

Doerne, G. Bruce and Richard W. Phidd Canadian Public Policy: Ideas, Structure, Process. Toronto: Methuen Publications, 1983.

Good, David A. The Politics of Anticipation: Making Canadian Federal Tax Policy. Ottawa: Carleton University School of Public Administration, 1980.

Kernaghan, W.D. Kenneth, ed. Public Administration in Canada: Selected Readings, 3rd Ed. Toronto: Methuen Press, 1977.

Langford, John W. The Question of Quangoes: Quasi-public Service Agencies in British Columbia. Canadian Public Administration. 26. (Winter 1983): 563-576.

Lindblom, Charles E. and David K. Cohen Usable Knowledge: Social Science and Social Problem Solving. New Haven: Yale University Press, 1979.

McCready, John. The Context for Canadian Social Policy: Values and Ideologies. Toronto: University of Toronto Press, 1981.

Mendelson, Michael. Universal or Selective? The Debate on Reforming Income Security in Canada. Toronto: Ontario Economic Council, Policy Study Series, 1981.

Newton, Mary J. Social Planning and Research Exchange System: 1983 Publications Catalogue. Toronto: Social Planning Council of Metropolitan Toronto, 1983.

Organization for Economic Cooperation and Development. The Welfare State in Crisis: An Account of the Conference on Social Policies in the 1980s, OECD Paris, 20-23 October, 1980. Paris: 1981.

Patton, Michael Quinn. Qualitative Evaluation Methods. Beverly Hills: Sage Publications, 1980.

Phillips, Bernard S. Social Research: Strategy and Tactics, 3rd Ed. New York: MacMillan Publishing Company Inc., 1976.

Prince, Michael J. and James Rice "Social Sectors and Social Policies", unpublished paper presented to the institute of Public Administration of Canada Conference at the Royal York Hotel. Toronto: September 1, 1982.

Pross, A. Paul Duality and Public Policy: A Conceptual Framework for Analyzing the Policy System of Atlantic Canada. Halifax: Institute of Public Affairs, Dalhousie University, 1980.

Pross, A. Paul, ed. Governing Under Pressure: The Special Interest Groups. Toronto: The Institute of Public Administration of Canada. 22 No. 2, Summer 1982.

Quebec. Commission d'enquete sur la santé et bien-être social. Les services sociaux: Rapport de la santé et bien-être social. Quatrième parte, volume VI. 1972.

Quebec. Commission of Inquiry on Health and Social Welfare (David Woodsworth and Patrick Deeby). Welfare Research on the Province of Quebec. Quebec: Quebec Official Publisher, R. Lefebvre, 1970.

Rasporich, A.W., ed. Social Sciences and Public Policy in Canada: Faculty of Social Sciences Inaugural Symposium Papers. Calgary, Alberta: Faculty of Social Sciences, University of Calgary, 1979.

Slayton, Philip and Michael J. Trebilcock, eds. The Professions and Public Policy, Conference of the Professions and Public Policy, University of Toronto, 1976. Toronto: University of Toronto Press, 1978.

Social Sciences and Humanities Research Council of Canada. Annual Report 1982-83. Ottawa: 1983.

Stacey, Margaret. methods of Social Research. Oxford: Pergamon Press, 1969.

Tropman, John G., J. Milan and Roger Lind, eds. New Strategic Perspectives on Social policy. New York: Pergamon Press, 1981.

Turner, Joanne C. and Francis J. Turner, eds. Canadian Social Welfare. Don Mills, Ontario: Collier MacMillan Canada Inc., 1981.

Watkins, Mary Michelle and James A. Ruffner, eds. Research Centres Directory, 1983. Detroit: Gale Research Co., 1983.

Wharf, Brian and Marilyn Callahan "Public Policy is a Voluntary Affair", BC Studies. 55 (Autumn 1982): 79-93.

Wharf, Brian and Allan Halladay The Role of Advisory Councils in Forming Social Policies, A Case Study of the National Council of Welfare. Hamilton, Ontario: McMaster University, School of Social Work, 1974.

Yelaja, Shankar A., ed. Canadian Social Policy. Waterloo, Ontario: Wilfred Laurier University Press, 1978.

MEMBERS OF THE INSTITUTE

Professor Kell Antoft
    Institute of Public Affairs
    Dalhousie University, Halifax
Marie-Andrée Bertrand
    École de criminologie
    Université de Montréal
Dr. Roger A. Blais
    École Polytechnique de Montréal
George Cooper, Q.C.
    McInnes, Cooper and Robertson, Halifax
James S. Cowan, Q.C.
    Partner, Stewart, MacKeen & Covert
    Halifax
V. Edward Daughney
    President, First City Trust Company
    Vancouver
Dr. Wendy Dobson
    Executive Director, C.D. Howe Institute
    Toronto
Marc Eliesen
    Chairperson
    Manitoba Energy Authority, Winnipeg
Emery Fanjoy
    Secretary, Council of Maritime Premiers
    Halifax
Dr. Allan K. Gillmore
    Executive Director, Association of
    Universities and Colleges of Canada,
    Ottawa
Dr. Donald Glendenning
    President, Holland College
    Charlottetown
Margaret C. Harris
    Past President, The National Council of
    Women of Canada, Saskatoon
Richard W. Johnston
    President, Spencer Stuart & Associates
    Toronto
Dr. Leon Katz, O.C.
    Saskatoon
Terrence Mactaggart
    Managing Director
    Sound Linked Data Inc., Mississauga
Dr. John S. McCallum
    Faculty of Administrative Studies
    University of Manitoba, Winnipeg
Claude Morin
    École nationale d'administration
    publique, Québec
Milan Nastich
    Canadian General Investments Limited
    Toronto
Professor William A. W. Neilson
    Dean, Faculty of Law
    University of Victoria
Roderick C. Nolan, P.Eng.
    Executive Vice-President
    Neill & Gunter Limited, Fredericton

Robert J. Olivero
    United Nations Secretariat, New York
Maureen O'Neil
    Co-ordinator, Status of Women Canada
    Ottawa
Garnet T. Page, O.C.
    Calgary
Dr. Gilles Paquet
    Dean, Faculty of Administration
    University of Ottawa
Dr. K. George Pedersen
    President
    University of Western Ontario
    London
Professor Marilyn L. Pilkington
    Osgoode Hall Law School, Toronto
Dr. David W. Slater
    Ottawa
Dr. Stuart L. Smith
    Chairman, Science Council of Canada
    Ottawa
Eldon D. Thompson
    President, Telesat, Vanier
Marc-Adélard Tremblay, O.C.
    Departement d'anthropologie
    Université Laval, Québec
Dr. Israel Unger
    Department of Chemistry
    University of New Brunswick
    Fredericton
Philip Vineberg, O.C., Q.C.
    Phillips & Vineberg, Montreal
Dr. Norman Wagner
    President, University of Calgary
Ida Wasacase, C.M.
    Winnipeg
Dr. R. Sherman Weaver
    Director
    Alberta Environmental Centre
    Vegreville
Dr. Blossom Wigdor
    Director, Program in Gerontology
    University of Toronto

Government Representatives
Herb Clarke, Newfoundland
Joseph H. Clarke, Nova Scotia
Michael Decter, Manitoba
Jim Dinning, Alberta
Hershell Ezrin, Ontario
Honourable Lowell Murray, Canada
John H. Parker, Northwest Territories
Henry Phillips, Prince Edward Island
Norman Riddell, Saskatchewan
Jean-K. Samson, Québec
Norman Spector, British Columbia
Eloise Spitzer, Yukon
Barry Toole, New Brunswick

INSTITUTE MANAGEMENT

Rod Dobell	President
Louis Vagianos	Special Assistant
Edgar Gallant	Fellow-in-Residence
Tom Kent	Fellow-in-Residence
Eric Kierans	Fellow-in-Residence
Jean-Luc Pepin	Fellow-in-Residence
Gordon Robertson	Fellow-in-Residence
Yvon Gasse	Director, Small and Medium-Sized Business Program
Barbara L. Hodgins	Director, Western Resources Program
Barry Lesser	Director, Regional Employment Opportunities Program
Frank Stone	A/Director, International Economics Program
Shirley Seward	Director, Co-ordination and Liaison
Parker Staples	Director, Financial Services & Treasurer
Donald Wilson	Director, Communications
Tom Kent	Editor, *Policy Options Politiques*

PUBLICATIONS AVAILABLE - MARCH 1986

Order Address:

The Institute for Research on Public Policy
P.O. Box 3670 South
Halifax, Nova Scotia
B3J 3K6

Leroy O. Stone & Claude Marceau	*Canadian Population Trends and Public Policy Through the 1980s.* 1977 $4.00
Raymond Breton	*The Canadian Condition: A Guide to Research in Public Policy.* 1977 $2.95
Raymond Breton	*Une orientation de la recherche politique dans le contexte canadien.* 1977 $2.95
J.W. Rowley & W.T. Stanbury (eds.)	*Competition Policy in Canada: Stage II, Bill C-13.* 1978 $12.95
C.F. Smart & W.T. Stanbury (eds.)	*Studies on Crisis Management.* 1978 $9.95
W.T. Stanbury (ed.)	*Studies on Regulation in Canada.* 1978 $9.95
Michael Hudson	*Canada in the New Monetary Order: Borrow? Devalue? Restructure!* 1978 $6.95
David K. Foot (ed.)	*Public Employment and Compensation in Canada: Myths and Realities.* 1978 $10.95
Raymond Breton & Gail Grant Akian	*Urban Institutions and People of Indian Ancestry: Suggestions for Research.* 1979 $3.00
Thomas H. Atkinson	*Trends in Life Satisfaction Among Canadians, 1968-1977.* 1979 $3.00
W.E. Cundiff & Mado Reid (eds.)	*Issues in Canadian/U.S. Transborder Computer Data Flows.* 1979 $6.50
Meyer W. Bucovetsky (ed.)	*Studies in Public Employment and Compensation in Canada.* 1979 $14.95
Richard French & André Béliveau	*The RCMP and the Management of National Security.* 1979 $6.95
Richard French & André Béliveau	*La GRC et la gestion de la sécurité nationale.* 1979 $6.95
G. Bruce Doern & Allan M. Maslove (eds.)	*The Public Evaluation of Government Spending.* 1979 $10.95

Leroy O. Stone & Michael J. MacLean	*Future Income Prospects for Canada's Senior Citizens.* 1979 $7.95
Richard M. Bird	*The Growth of Public Employment in Canada.* 1979 $12.95
Richard J. Schultz	*Federalism and the Regulatory Process.* 1979 $1.50
Richard J. Schultz	*Le fédéralisme et le processus de réglementation.* 1979 $1.50
Lionel D. Feldman & Katherine A. Graham	*Bargaining for Cities, Municipalities and Intergovernmental Relations: An Assessment.* 1979 $10.95
Elliot J. Feldman & Neil Nevitte (eds.)	*The Future of North America: Canada, the United States, and Quebec Nationalism.* 1979 $7.95
David R. Protheroe	*Imports and Politics: Trade Decision Making in Canada, 1968-1979.* 1980 $8.95
G. Bruce Doern	*Government Intervention in the Canadian Nuclear Industry.* 1980 $8.95
G. Bruce Doern & Robert W. Morrison (eds.)	*Canadian Nuclear Policies.* 1980 $14.95
Allan M. Maslove & Gene Swimmer	*Wage Controls in Canada: 1975-78: A Study of Public Decision Making.* 1980 $11.95
T. Gregory Kane	*Consumers and the Regulators: Intervention in the Federal Regulatory Process.* 1980 $10.95
Réjean Lachapelle & Jacques Henripin	*La situation démolinguistique au Canada: évolution passée et prospective.* 1980 $24.95
Albert Breton & Anthony Scott	*The Design of Federations.* 1980 $6.95
A.R. Bailey & D.G. Hull	*The Way Out: A More Revenue-Dependent Public Sector and How It Might Revitalize the Process of Governing.* 1980 $6.95
David R. Harvey	*Christmas Turkey or Prairie Vulture? An Economic Analysis of the Crow's Nest Pass Grain Rates.* 1980 $10.95
Donald G. Cartwright	*Official Language Populations in Canada: Patterns and Contacts.* 1980 $4.95
Richard M. Bird	*Taxing Corporations.* 1980 $6.95
Leroy O. Stone & Susan Fletcher	*A Profile of Canada's Older Population.* 1980 $7.95
Peter N. Nemetz (ed.)	*Resource Policy: International Perspectives.* 1980 $18.95
Keith A.J. Hay (ed.)	*Canadian Perspectives on Economic Relations With Japan.* 1980 $18.95
Dhiru Patel	*Dealing With Interracial Conflict: Policy Alternatives.* 1980 $5.95

Raymond Breton & Gail Grant	*La langue de travail au Québec : synthèse de la recherche sur la rencontre de deux langues.* 1981 $10.95
Diane Vanasse	*L'évolution de la population scolaire du Québec.* 1981 $12.95
David M. Cameron (ed.)	*Regionalism and Supranationalism: Challenges and Alternatives to the Nation-State in Canada and Europe.* 1981 $9.95
Heather Menzies	*Women and the Chip: Case Studies of the Effects of Information on Employment in Canada.* 1981 $8.95
H.V. Kroeker (ed.)	*Sovereign People or Sovereign Governments.* 1981 $12.95
Peter Aucoin (ed.)	*The Politics and Management of Restraint in Government.* 1981 $17.95
Nicole S. Morgan	*Nowhere to Go? Possible Consequences of the Demographic Imbalance in Decision-Making Groups of the Federal Public Service.* 1981 $8.95
Nicole S. Morgan	*Où aller? Les conséquences prévisibles des déséquilibres démographiques chez les groupes de décision de la fonction publique fédérale.* 1981 $8.95
Raymond Breton, Jeffrey G. Reitz & Victor F. Valentine	*Les frontières culturelles et la cohésion du Canada.* 1981 $18.95
Peter N. Nemetz (ed.)	*Energy Crisis: Policy Response.* 1981 $10.95
James Gillies	*Where Business Fails.* 1981 $9.95
Allan Tupper & G. Bruce Doern (eds.)	*Public Corporations and Public Policy in Canada.* 1981 $16.95
Réjean Lachapelle & Jacques Henripin	*The Demolinguistic Situation in Canada: Past Trends and Future Prospects.* 1982 $24.95
Irving Brecher	*Canada's Competition Policy Revisited: Some New Thoughts on an Old Story.* 1982 $3.00
Ian McAllister	*Regional Development and the European Community: A Canadian Perspective.* 1982 $13.95
Donald J. Daly	*Canada in an Uncertain World Economic Environment.* 1982 $3.00
W.T. Stanbury & Fred Thompson	*Regulatory Reform in Canada.* 1982 $7.95
Robert J. Buchan, C. Christopher Johnston, T. Gregory Kane, Barry Lesser, Richard J. Schultz & W.T. Stanbury	*Telecommunications Regulation and the Constitution.* 1982 $18.95
Rodney de C. Grey	*United States Trade Policy Legislation: A Canadian View.* 1982 $7.95
John Quinn & Philip Slayton (eds.)	*Non-Tariff Barriers After the Tokyo Round.* 1982 $17.95

Stanley M. Beck & Ivan Bernier (eds.)	*Canada and the New Constitution: The Unfinished Agenda.* 2 vols. 1983 $10.95 (set)
R. Brian Woodrow & Kenneth B. Woodside (eds.)	*The Introduction of Pay-TV in Canada: Issues and Implications.* 1983 $14.95
E.P. Weeks & L. Mazany	*The Future of the Atlantic Fisheries.* 1983 $5.00
Douglas D. Purvis (ed.), assisted by Frances Chambers	*The Canadian Balance of Payments: Perspectives and Policy Issues.* 1983 $24.95
Roy A. Matthews	*Canada and the "Little Dragons": An Analysis of Economic Developments in Hong Kong, Taiwan, and South Korea and the Challenge/Opportunity They Present for Canadian Interests in the 1980s.* 1983 $11.95
Charles Pearson & Gerry Salembier	*Trade, Employment, and Adjustment.* 1983 $5.00
Steven Globerman	*Cultural Regulation in Canada.* 1983 $11.95
F.R. Flatters & R.G. Lipsey	*Common Ground for the Canadian Common Market.* 1983 $5.00
Frank Bunn, assisted by U. Domb, D. Huntley, H. Mills, H. Silverstein	*Oceans from Space: Towards the Management of Our Coastal Zones.* 1983 $5.00
C.D. Shearing & P.C. Stenning	*Private Security and Private Justice: The Challenge of the 80s.* 1983 $5.00
Jacob Finkelman & Shirley B. Goldenberg	*Collective Bargaining in the Public Service: The Federal Experience in Canada.* 2 vols. 1983 $29.95 (set)
Gail Grant	*The Concrete Reserve: Corporate Programs for Indians in the Urban Work Place.* 1983 $5.00
Owen Adams & Russell Wilkins	*Healthfulness of Life.* 1983 $8.00
Yoshi Tsurumi with Rebecca R. Tsurumi	*Sogoshosha: Engines of Export-Based Growth.* (Revised Edition). 1984 $10.95
Raymond Breton & Gail Grant (eds.)	*The Dynamics of Government Programs for Urban Indians in the Prairie Provinces.* 1984 $19.95
Frank Stone	*Canada, The GATT and the International Trade System.* 1984 $15.00
Pierre Sauvé	*Private Bank Lending and Developing-Country Debt.* 1984 $10.00
Mark Thompson & Gene Swimmer	*Conflict or Compromise: The Future of Public Sector Industrial Relations.* 1984 $15.00
Samuel Wex	*Instead of FIRA: Autonomy for Canadian Subsidiaries?* 1984 $8.00
R.J. Wonnacott	*Selected New Developments in International Trade Theory.* 1984 $7.00
R.J. Wonnacott	*Aggressive US Reciprocity Evaluated with a New Analytical Approach to Trade Conflicts.* 1984 $8.00

Richard W. Wright	*Japanese Business in Canada: The Elusive Alliance.* 1984 $12.00
Paul K. Gorecki & W.T. Stanbury	*The Objectives of Canadian Competition Policy, 1888-1983.* 1984 $15.00
Michael Hart	*Some Thoughts on Canada-United States Sectoral Free Trade.* 1985 $7.00
J. Peter Meekison Roy J. Romanow & William D. Moull	*Origins and Meaning of Section 92A: The 1982 Constitutional Amendment on Resources.* 1985 $10.00
Conference Papers	*Canada and International Trade. Volume One: Major Issues of Canadian Trade Policy. Volume Two: Canada and the Pacific Rim.* 1985 $25.00 (set)
A.E. Safarian	*Foreign Direct Investment: A Survey of Canadian Research.* 1985 $8.00
Joseph R. D'Cruz & James D. Fleck	*Canada Can Compete! Strategic Management of the Canadian Industrial Portfolio.* 1985 $18.00
Barry Lesser & Louis Vagianos	*Computer Communications and the Mass Market in Canada.* 1985 $10.00
W.R. Hines	*Trade Policy Making in Canada: Are We Doing it Right?* 1985 $10.00
Bertrand Nadeau	*Britain's Entry into the European Economic Community and its Effect on Canada's Agricultural Exports.* 1985 $10.00
Paul B. Huber	*Promoting Timber Cropping: Policies Toward Non-Industrial Forest Owners in New Brunswick.* 1985 $10.00
Gordon Robertson	*Northern Provinces: A Mistaken Goal.* 1985 $8.00
Petr Hanel	*La technologie et les exportations canadiennes du matériel pour la filière bois-papier.* 1985 $20.00
Marc Malone	*Une place pour le Québec au Canada.* 1986 $20.00
Russel M. Wills, Steven Globerman & Peter J. Booth	*Software Policies for Growth and Export.* 1986 $15.00
A. R. Dobell & S. H. Mansbridge	*The Social Policy Process in Canada.* 1986 $8.00